Take
Care of

MAY 07

 Way™

OCT 09 2000

Take Care of Your Car

Michael and Carol Kennedy

Macmillan • USA

To my wife Carol, my daughter Kara, and to my mother who taught me everything about honesty, integrity and the meaning of hard work.

G.M.K.

Macmillan Publishing books may be purchased for business or sales promotional use. For information please write: Special Markets Department, Macmillan Publishing USA, 1633 Broadway, New York, NY 10019.

International Standard Book Number: 0-02-862647-8
Library of Congress Catalog Card Number: 98-88083

00 99 98   8 7 6 5 4 3 2 1

Interpretation of the printing code: the rightmost number of the first series of numbers is the year of the book's printing; the rightmost number of the second series of numbers is the number of the book's printing. For example, a printing code of 98-1 shows that the first printing occurred in 1998.

Printed in the United States of America

Book Design: Madhouse Studios

Page creation by Carrie Allen, Eric Brinkman, and Heather Pope.

You Don't Have to Feel Guilty Anymore!

IT'S O.K. TO DO IT *THE LAZY WAY*!

It seems every time we turn around, we're given more responsibility, more information to absorb, more places we need to go, and more numbers, dates, and names to remember. Both our bodies and our minds are already on overload. And we know what happens next—cleaning the house, balancing the checkbook, and cooking dinner get put off until "tomorrow" and eventually fall by the wayside.

So let's be frank—we're all starting to feel a bit guilty about the dirty laundry, stacks of ATM slips, and Chinese take-out. Just thinking about tackling those terrible tasks makes you exhausted, right? If only there were an easy, effortless way to get this stuff done! (And done right!)

There is—*The Lazy Way*! By providing the pain-free way to do something—including tons of shortcuts and time-saving tips, as well as lists of all the stuff you'll ever need to get it done efficiently—*The Lazy Way* series cuts through all of the time-wasting thought processes and laborious exercises. You'll discover the secrets of those who have figured out *The Lazy Way*. You'll get things done in half the time it takes the average person—and then you will sit back and smugly consider those poor suckers who haven't discovered *The Lazy Way* yet. With *The Lazy Way,* you'll learn how to put in minimal effort and get maximum results so you can devote your attention and energy to the pleasures in life!

THE LAZY WAY PROMISE

Everyone on *The Lazy Way* staff promises that, if you adopt *The Lazy Way* philosophy, you'll never break a sweat, you'll barely lift a finger, you won't put strain on your brain, and you'll have plenty of time to put up your feet. We guarantee you will find that these activities are no longer hardships, since you're doing them *The Lazy Way*. We also firmly support taking breaks and encourage rewarding yourself (we even offer our suggestions in each book!). With *The Lazy Way*, the only thing you'll be overwhelmed by is all of your newfound free time!

THE LAZY WAY SPECIAL FEATURES

Every book in our series features the following sidebars in the margins, all designed to save you time and aggravation down the road.

- **"Quick n' Painless"**—shortcuts that get the job done fast.
- **"You'll Thank Yourself Later"**—advice that saves time down the road.
- **"A Complete Waste of Time"**—warnings that spare countless headaches and squandered hours.
- **"If You're So Inclined"**—optional tips for moments of inspired added effort.
- **"The Lazy Way"**—rewards to make the task more pleasurable.

If you've either decided to give up altogether or have taken a strong interest in the subject, you'll find information on hiring outside help with "How to Get Someone Else to Do It" as well as further reading recommendations in "If You Want to Learn More, Read These." In addition, there's an only-what-you-need-to-know glossary of terms and product names ("If You Don't Know What It Means/Does, Look Here") as well as "It's Time for Your Reward"—fun and relaxing ways to treat yourself for a job well done.

With *The Lazy Way* series, you'll find that getting the job done has never been so painless!

Series Editor
Amy Gordon

Managing Editor
Robert Shuman

Editorial Director
Gary Krebs

Director of Creative Services
Michele Laseau

Development Editor
Alana Morgan

Cover Designer
Michael Freeland

Production Editor
Carol Sheehan

What's in This Book

If You Feel As If Your Car Has Been Running Your Life, It's Time to Turn the Tables!

If you feel as though your car has been running your life, it's time to turn the tables! Sure, some people out there spend every waking moment hovering over their cars or under a lift tinkering with them. But if you've got a busy life like the rest of us, who's got the time for that?

On the other hand, you probably don't have time to wait by the side of the road for the tow truck to come along and drag you to the repair shop either. There should be a happy medium—and there is. In the following chapters, we'll show you how you can spend a few moments up front before things go wrong and still have time to live the rest of your life outside the confines of your garage.

In this book, we've divided everything up into three easy sections to make it simple for you to find the stuff you need right away. Because good organization is the ultimate lazy way, we've started out in Parts 1 and 2 discussing what tools you need (and what you could do without!), how to organize them, and how to use them—in other words, what maintenance you need to do, when you need to do it, what you can skip over, and what you can turn over to your repair shop (the ultimate in lazy!). In Part 3, we get into the basics of keeping your car running, from transmission to tailpipes and everything in between. Just in case you don't read all that, we end the part by discussing how to handle the stuff that goes wrong once you leave the garage and go out onto the open road.

Finally, when you don't have the time or the expertise to do it yourself, we show you how to find the best place to have somebody else do it for you and what resources can help you in your quest to maintain your car *The Lazy Way*!

Thank You...

A special thanks to all those car-care professionals who volunteered their advice and information to assist us. Thanks, too, to our agent Bert Holtje and our editors Alana Morgan and Amy Gordon.

G.M.K. and C.K.

Part 1

The Painless Garage

Are You Too Lazy to Read The Painless Garage?

1 The only things you can find in your glove compartment are a pair of socks, a guide to the 1988 Vancouver World's Fair, and a day-old Twinkie. ☐ yes ☐ no

2 Your idea of a set of car tools is a bent coat hanger and a couple of rubber bands. ☐ yes ☐ no

3 The best place to find car supplies is in your neighbor's garage. ☐ yes ☐ no

Chapter one

The Tidy Toolbox

We'll be saying this over and over in this book—you need to take your car to a skilled mechanic for major repairs. Who has the time to do those big repairs anyway, even if you knew how? But for all the little things that you can do to save you time and trouble down the line, you need the right tool. Yes, you really do.

If you've ever tried to open a locked car door with a coat hanger, you know what we mean—a key is a lot more efficient, because it's designed to do the job. The right tool makes the job go quicker. Having the right tools doesn't mean you have to go out spend more on tools than you did for the car you're going to be working on. Most maintenance jobs that you can tackle on your own can be done with just a few good tools.

MANUALS

The most important tools you can get don't come with shiny metal handles—they're the owner's and service manuals for your particular type of car. Before you even think about

QUICK 🄝 PAINLESS

picking up a spark plug, get your owner's manual out of the glove compartment and read it. It should tell you what needs to be done at each scheduled maintenance visit. After you've digested all the good stuff in there, you can move on to the service manual.

Service manuals don't come automatically packaged in the glove compartment, but you can buy one from any dealer's parts department or by contacting the manufacturer. If you have a computer, you'll find that most are also available for purchase online. Although there are many manuals on the market, it's wise to stick to a well-known type, produced either by the manufacturer or an auto publisher such as Chilton, Mitchell, or Robert Bentley. You should be able to get the same manuals that the technicians use. There are certainly jobs in there you won't want to tackle yourself, but the specific, basic stuff will come in handy.

IN THE TOOLBOX

Look over the following lists. If you're just starting out and you try to buy all of these things at once, you'll find yourself forking over quite a pile of change. But when you consider how much your car cost in the first place, spending a few hundred dollars to keep it running in tip-top condition isn't so outrageous. Spread out the cost by buying the tools as you need them. Odds are, you probably already have at least some of these important devices lying around under the dog food bowl or stashed behind the that pile of window screens.

Must Haves

Here are the tools you really need to stock up on if you're going to do any work on your car:

- Antifreeze tester
- Battery cleaner tool
- Pliers (arc joint)
- Pliers (8-inch slip joint)
- Pliers (diagonal-cutting)
- Pliers (needle-nose)
- Pliers (vise-grip)
- Screwdrivers (standard)
- Screwdrivers (Phillips head)
- Wrench set (Allen)
- Wrench set (open-end)
- Wrench set (box end or combination wrench set)
- Wrench (Crescent, adjustable wrench)
- Socket wrench set
- Ratchets and extension bars
- Spark plug socket wrench
- Ball peen hammer

Not a Bad Idea

Now that you've got your basics stowed away safely in your toolbox, consider the following—they'll come in handy, although they're not essential:

Congratulations! You've read your owner's manual! Now take a break and go watch some reruns of *My Mother the Car.*

The Lazy Way

IF YOU'RE SO
INCLINED

Buy wrenches and sock-ets in sets to save money; you can always add to the set later if you need to.

- Feeler gauges (flat and wire type)
- Files
- Funnel
- Gasket scraper
- Rubber mallet
- Filter wrench
- Tire gauge
- Hack saw

For the Truly Committed

You'll only need to buy the following tools if you're obsessed with taking care of your car—or you're plan-ning on becoming a full-time mechanic:

- Torque wrench
- Pullers
- Set of chisels and punches
- Hydrometer
- Compression gauge
- Digital multimeter

IN THE GARAGE

Now that you've got your toolbox in order, it's time to look around your garage to see if you've stocked up on the essentials: some basic equipment to help make your life easier if you're planning on working on your own car.

Must Haves

No matter what, there are just a few items you've really *got* to have if you don't want to drive yourself crazy. They'll make your life easier, and they're essential for *The Lazy Way:*

- Flashlight
- Safety glasses or goggles (always use them when you work with a hammer and chisel or punches)
- Pan for catching oil or antifreeze

Not a Bad Idea

Okay, we admit it—you don't *have* to have the following items on hand in order to work on your car, but they'll sure make your life a lot easier if you do:

- Hydraulic jack
- Jack stands or ramps
- Pry bar

For the Truly Committed

If you're the type of person who likes to cover up your car whenever you're not driving it, you're probably the type of person who's going to want to do everything by the book. The following items aren't required, but gee, they're sure nice to have!

- Fender cover (rubber is nice)
- Magnet (long and narrow)

QUICK ⬭ PAINLESS

Don't forget to have "convenience" items such as drip pans and funnels on hand. They'll make working on your car much easier and more comfortable.

The 3 Worst Things to Do with Your Washer Solvent Container:

1. Put water into the container (especially in winter).

2. Put dish detergent into the container (it will leave a film).

3. Put radiator antifreeze into the container (this will damage your washer system and ruin the car's paint job).

CLEANING SUPPLIES

The best tools and equipment in the world won't help if your car is a gunky mess, so now it's time to check over your cleaning supplies to make sure you've stocked up on the basics.

Must Haves

If you want to do the best cleaning with the least amount of effort, you've got to have the right products to help you. Check to make sure you've got these essentials:

- Armor All
- Laundry detergent
- Old towels
- Car parts cleaning solvent
- Scrub brush (gentle bristles)
- Wax
- Windshield washer solvent

Not a Bad Idea

These cleaning supplies are nice, but the world isn't going to come to a screeching halt if you don't have them:

- Carpet cleaner
- Latex gloves
- Cat litter (standard clay)
- Chamois

- Hand cleaner (pumice soaps, borax, and so on)
- Upholstery cleaner (spray-on)
- Aerosol-type foam automotive glass cleaner

For the Truly Committed

A few of these cleaning products really aren't necessary unless you like to get particular about how you clean your car:

- Squeegee
- "Liquid" or "invisible" gloves

OTHER SUPPLIES

There are a range of car-care products that you'll need to have on hand to help your car run better, such as antifreeze, engine oil, and so on. Read on to find out what you do and don't need.

Must Haves

There are some products that you just can't live without. No matter how lazy you're feeling, run out and buy these if you don't already have them in your garage:

- Antifreeze
- WD-40 penetrating oil in spray can
- Carburetor cleaner
- Brake cleaner
- Oil for lubricating
- Touch-up paint in correct shade
- White grease in spray can

YOU'LL THANK YOURSELF LATER

Solvents are flammable. Store solvents and soaked rags in a metal can with a tight lid, away from flames, sparks, electric light switches, and space and water heaters.

While some people may be perfectly content to only clean their car once a month, some of us are not so relaxed . . . so if you like to take things a step further, invest in some Scotchguard™ for your seat covers and stop fretting about food droppings!

Not a Bad Idea

Here are a couple of products that can make your life easier, but don't go crazy if you don't have these in stock:

- Grease cartridge for grease gun
- White grease in spray can
- Touch-up paint in correct shade

For the Truly Committed

Sure, you could probably go your whole life without the following items, but for those of us who live on the finicky side of life, here are some products that will help keep your car in great shape with very little effort!

- Contact spray
- Parts washer
- Wheel cleaners
- Scotchgard™ for seat covers
- Silver polish

CAN'T-MISS EQUIPMENT

A few larger pieces of equipment can make your car-care jobs go quicker and easier. Check the following lists to see how your garage stacks up.

Must Haves

Don't even think about fixing your own car unless you've got some of these items:

- Grease gun
- Jumper cables

- Floor jacks
- Jack stand

Not a Bad Idea

These two items can take the agony out of car care—and save lots of time, too:

- Fluorescent trouble light (or drop light)
- Shop vacuum

For the Truly Committed

If you're just dying to have a well-equipped garage like the pros, check out these items:

- Creeper
- Drive-up ramps
- Tachometer

WHERE TO STOCK UP ON YOUR STUFF

Now that you've read through the lists of equipment, tools and supplies, there are probably a few items you're missing. Now is the time to stock up—*before* you're in the middle of a job and suddenly realize you don't have the very piece of equipment you need to do the job. That's a real time-waster. Read on to find out where to purchase your supplies.

Basic Supplies

You can get a lot of your supplies, such as oil, just about any place, from the corner drug store to a large discount department store or a car parts place. You can also find

Congratulations! You've read through the list of tools you'll need. Now go take a nap and rest up before you go out to buy the tools you don't have yet.

The Lazy Way

QUICK *n* PAINLESS

Buy a couple of jugs of washer solvent and antifreeze *now* and keep yourself ahead of the game!

jugs of washer solvent and antifreeze at these stores. Look for the sales and pick up a couple of jugs for rock-bottom prices.

Tool Time

The most important thing to consider when buying tools is the tool's quality. Don't be misled by the low cost of bargain tools, such as those advertised in the "200 tools for $29" ads you've seen in discount catalogs. Remember, when you buy a cheap tool, you're getting what you pay for.

If you're a tool snob, you can buy top-of-the-line tools like the pros use at an independent dealer such as Snap-On or Mac. These dealers sell most of their products to mechanics, but you can certainly contact either one and buy your tools from them. Most tools sold by these dealers come with a lifetime warranty, no questions asked.

If you're more the Toyota than the Testarossa type, you can get medium-priced, good-quality tools such as SK at an auto parts supply house or at a department store such as Sears (which sells its own line of Craftsman tools with a lifetime warranty). If you tend to fling your tools at the cat and bend your wrenches into pretzels, you might want to think about patronizing a place such as Sears, where you can get a tool replaced more readily than at an auto parts store.

If you like the idea of doing some of your own car repairs (the easy ones that save you time down the road), it can be cheaper to buy a complete mechanic's set of tools. Look for sales at large department stores or hardware stores, and check out the want ads in newspapers for used sets.

Parts

There are three places to go when you look for parts: authorized dealers, auto supply and chain/department stores, and used part stores or salvage yards. Some kinds of parts sell very well and are easy to find (such as spark plugs, belts, hoses, and so on). Other types of parts may be very specific or trim pieces and may be moldering on a shelf for years before a buyer comes along. You'll have to visit a dealer for these parts.

Authorized dealers are licensed to sell certain brands of new cars, and they must invest money to buy and stock replacement parts. Dealers must carry (or be able to order) any part that can be found on certain models within the line. Dealers all charge about the same, which is the full list price for parts, although some places will give you a small discount from time to time. Dealers sell OEM (original equipment manufactured) parts; these parts are the best quality and will work as they are intended. They will usually be more expensive than other parts, but they usually come with a 12 months/12,000-mile warranty. If you want reliability, accuracy, warranty, and quality, then OEM parts are the way to go.

Some of the parts you may find in an auto supply store may be even better than the OEM part. Shopping around at several auto parts stores may help you save a good deal of money. Franchised chain auto parts stores often have excellent values and low prices, and major retail chain stores also have complete parts facilities.

YOU'LL THANK YOURSELF LATER

Call first! Always check to find out who has the part you need before you leave the house and save yourself a lot of time and aggravation!

If you're looking for a bargain, you can head for the used parts and salvage yards. Salvage companies buy wrecked cars from insurance companies or older, non-running cars. However, you won't get guarantees here, and you may have no idea about whether the used part you're getting at a salvage yard may be more badly worn than the original part you're replacing.

For some parts, rebuilt items can be a good buy, such as rebuilt alternators and starters. Many times, these rebuilt items are almost as good as new.

We all like to save money, but stay away from *gypsy parts,* which are counterfeit auto parts whose boxes are designed to mimic the better-made, more expensive brand names. If you have any doubts, ask the parts manager at your shop what parts they use. Some repair shops may unknowingly use counterfeit parts. It pays to ask.

Equipment

Tires are one of the most important safety devices you can buy, and if you do the job right the first time, you won't need to keep going back to replace your tires. When buying new tires, keep these tips in mind:

- All four tires should be the same construction (radial, bias, or bias-belted). Never mix tire types. Ever!

- The wheels should be the correct width for the tires (check the charts at the tire dealer); a mismatch can cause sloppy handling and rapid tread wear.

- Never mount a regular tire on a special spare wheel.

- Make sure the tires don't touch the car's body when the car is heavily loaded, hits bumps, or makes a hard turn.

QUICK n' PAINLESS

The best place to find parts for older cars is though *Hemming's Motor News,* the car restorer's bible. You can buy a copy at any newsstand or call (802) 442-3101.

Getting Time on Your Side

	The Old Way	The Lazy Way
Finding the tool you need	Days	2 minutes
Figuring out which tool you need	Months	5 minutes
Protecting your car while you work on it	Oops!	2 seconds
Keeping your work area clean	What?! It's a garage!	As you go!
Reading your manual	Not until it's too late	30 minutes and now you're ahead of the game!
Finding the part you need	7 trips	1 trip (you knew where to go first!)

Chapter two

Information Please!

If you don't have lots of time to spend asking questions of your mechanic, you may find that surfing the Net is an easier and quicker way to get car information. This chapter tells you where to find the best sites.

EXPERT ORGANIZATIONS

AAA has always been considered one of the best organizations for the car owner, and they're everywhere that you are! Check out the site below to find information on your local association.

American Automobile Association (AAA)
http://www.aaa.com

SAFETY FIRST!

When you really think about it, you're putting a lot of trust in your car every time you drive yourself and your loved ones somewhere. Take advantage of these valuable sites so you can stay up to date on the latest safety issues.

QUICK ⁿ PAINLESS

You trust them to tow your car and handle other car issues. So, try American Automobile Association's Web site first (on p. 17), and trust them to answer all your car maintenance questions!

American Auto Manufacturer's Association
http://www.aama.com

This site contains industry data, safety information, news, and links to related sites.

National Highway Traffic Safety Administration
http://www.nhtsa.dot.gov

This site has safety news, links to related sites, recall information, ratings, a driving simulator, and vehicle and equipment information.

FOR THE CONSUMER

Before you buy, compare! Check out these sites to make sure you're getting a good deal, and don't forget them if you're selling either!

Autobody Online
http://www.autobodyonline.com

On this page, you'll find links to various organizations that oversee the business practices of body shops.

Autoconnect: Compare New and Used Cars
http://209.143.231.6

Use this site to compare data on new and used cars.

Edmunds Consumer Information/Edmunds Buyers' Guides
http://www.edmunds.com

This site provides new and used car prices and other information.

Kelley Blue Book

http://www.kbb.com

This site lists car prices and links to related sites.

NEED A PART?

Where to go? Who to ask? Before you canvas the city looking for that one crucial part, scan these sites first and arm yourself with information!

Automatic Transmission Rebuilders Association

http://www.atra-gears.com

This site provides consumer information about transmissions.

Automotive Parts and Accessories Association

http://www.apaa.org

This site is a good source for after-market information.

TIPS, TRICKS, AND SHORTCUTS FROM THE EXPERTS!

Got the parts you need but not sure of where to start? Need a hand troubleshooting a squeek, bang or crunch? Take a look at these sites and see what other people have already discovered. Odds are you're not the first person dealing with the car problem in front of you!

Automotive Service Association

http://www.asashop.org

This site provides a newsletter, maintenance tips, and guidelines for finding a good repair shop.

IF YOU'RE SO
INCLINED

Curious about the latest changes in safety regulations? Check out the National Highway Traffic Safety Administration's site (on p. 18) and stay up to date!

AutoShop Online

http://www.autoshop-online.com

This automotive diagnostic service for consumers on the Internet also provides travel and auto tips.

Autosite Report

http://www.autosite.com

Everything you ever wanted to know about car repairs is on this site. You can also find car words that you may not understand in the auto repair encyclopedia.

Car Care Corner

http://www.peoplevision.com/carcare/corner.htm

This site provides maintenance and repair tips for motorists, current articles and updates, and links to related sites.

National Institute for Automotive Service Excellence

http://www.asecert.org

You can find tips for motorists, racing info, links to related sites, and certification details at this site.

HEAR ALL ABOUT IT! NEWSFLASH!

This site will keep you in the know about the latest information out there, so stop in every so often and stay on top of the car industry!

YOU'LL THANK YOURSELF LATER

Not sure whether to buy old or new? Check out Autoconnect's site (on p. 18) and compare for yourself before you put any money down!

Auto.Com

http://www.auto.com

You'll find car repair links, news, stock information, and more at this site.

ASK THE EXPERTS!

Got a problem that you can't seem to find the answer to? Curious about something? Tap into these experts! E-mail them your queries and they'll fill you in!

The C.A.R. Show

http://www.thecarshow.com

E-mail your automotive questions to show host Roger Kwapich.

Cartalk

http://www.cartalk.com

This site is the place to connect with *Cartalk,* with hosts Tom and Ray Magliozzi. You can read their columns, e-mail questions, or link to related sites.

Nutz & Boltz

http://www.nutzandboltz.com

This site is the home of the *Nutz & Boltz Show* and newsletter.

A COMPLETE WASTE OF TIME

The 3 Worst Things You Can Do when Doing Your Own Car Maintenance:

1. Don't ask an expert when you're not sure what to do.

2. Assume that the old "Do It Yourself" book about cars is still accurate.

3. Neglect the vast resources that are at your fingertips on the Internet.

GENERAL INFORMATION

Whether it's maintenance tips, information databases, or consumer information you seek, these places should be tops on your list.

Auto Channel
http://www.theautochannel.com

This site is the Internet's most complete and comprehensive listing of motorspots and automotive information resources; it includes streaming audio, video, and a wide variety of free databases.

Car Care Council
http://www.carcarecouncil.org

This site provides information on maintenance, national car care month, women-related issues, and the *C.A.R.* radio show. It also provides links to related sites.

eAuto
http://www.eauto.com

The eAuto site is everything automotive; it's the most comprehensive Internet-based resource for automotive information.

Mister Fixit
http://www.misterfixit.com/autorepr.htm

Go to this site to find everything you need to know about your car.

QUICK 🔘 PAINLESS

A pit stop on the Web can cut down on pit stops for your car, so sit back, have a cup of coffee and do some preventative browsing online!

Professional Master Technicians Association

http://www.rowriter.com/pmta/

This site for the Professional Master Technicians Association has links to related sites and other data.

Woman Motorist

http://www.womanmotorist.com

The first all-woman Internet site for women motorists has car reviews, safety information, car shopping advice, maintenance tips, and more.

Congratulations! You've spent some valuable time to get the answers you need. Now find the nearest comfy chair and take a nap! You deserve it!

The Lazy Way

Getting Time On Your Side

	The Old Way	The Lazy Way
Getting the right part	8 tries	1 trip
Troubleshooting a noise	Could be days	30 minutes, on the Net!
Getting the lowdown on that used car you're thinking about buying for your kid	Not until after you've paid for it	20 minutes
Making sure you get a fair deal on your trade-in	Never	20 minutes
Getting the latest recall information for your car	Weeks	20 minutes
Finding answers to your transmission questions	Days	20 minutes

Part 2

Keeping Things Running Like a Well-Oiled Machine

Are You Too Lazy to Read Keeping Things Running Like a Well-Oiled Machine?

1 The last time you cleaned your car, Edsels were rolling off the Ford assembly line. ☐ yes ☐ no

2 You don't keep track of your maintenance schedule because you don't maintain your car, and you don't maintain your car because you don't have a maintenance schedule. ☐ yes ☐ no

3 It's much easier to go buy a new tool when you need it than to dig out the garage to find the old one. ☐ yes ☐ no

Chapter three

Organize and Minimize

Now that you know what tools you should already have, you need to learn how to keep them organized. It may seem like it's easier to leave them right where you dropped them the last time you worked on the car. Or maybe you've gotten into the bad habit of tossing your tools onto a workbench until by the end of the day your garage looks more like a going-out-of-business sale at a hardware store.

Odds are, if you leave your tools right where you drop them, they are going to get lost, dirty, rusted, or broken. Then the next time you suddenly have to change a tire, you won't be able to find your lug wrench. Because the last time you used your lug wrench you were also watching the British Grand Prix on your garage portable TV with the little tiny black-and-white screen, and you got excited, and…well, that's the last time you saw that wrench. So it takes you 25 minutes of searching before you unearth it. Now, that's not *The Lazy Way* to maintain your car.

A GARAGE YOU CAN WORK IN

Before you start organizing your tools, take a look around. Most folks store their car tools, and their car, in the garage. But your garage may not be the clean, bright place it should be. If your garage is a storage bin for all the junk you don't have room for in your house, think seriously about taking a weekend and clearing everything out.

It will be much easier to find things if there's a place to put them, and much easier to have a place to put them if you get rid of all those lava lamps, inflatable boats, and 40 years' worth of *National Geographics* that are taking up valuable garage space. An orderly garage can make a big difference in your life! Apply the same organization skills you use inside the house to clear up clutter in the garage and make it a pleasant place to putter.

Clean Up and Look Up

As you begin solving the garage storage problem, think "clean up and look up." You can use overhead storage (shelves, platforms, cabinets, ledges) to create additional floor space for a car work space.

Take a look at available space all around. How high is the roof? Is it flat or peaked? How much space does your car need, not only in length, but in height, too? You're in luck if your one-car garage has a peaked roof. Gable and hip roofs are terrific for storage. Shed-roof structures also provide some overhead space between the rafters and ceiling line. In a flat-roofed garage, you've only got the space between the top of your head or vehicle and the ceiling.

Ventilate and Illuminate

To prevent the buildup of moisture, auto exhaust, paint fumes, or shop dust in a closed garage, ventilation is a necessity. As a rule, there should be 1 square foot of open vent space per 150 square feet of floor area.

Ideally, you should mix natural and artificial light. Overhead fluorescent shop units are the most efficient for general artificial lighting; one 4-foot, double-tube shop unit lights up about 40 square feet. Paint the walls and ceiling of the garage a white or a light color to amplify light by reflection. Using enamel paint will make the walls easier to clean.

STORAGE UNITS

Because most storage problems stem from a lack of floor space, it's a good idea to raise storage units above the ground whenever possible. You can hang them high on a wall or suspend them from the rafters or joists. Built-in storage space can make a big difference in your garage. Consider installing some of the following:

- Floor-to-ceiling shelves on the inside wall
- A continuous, two-foot-deep shelf running around three sides of the garage
- A four-foot shelf above the garage doors for extra-deep storage

A COMPLETE WASTE OF TIME

The 3 Worst Things to Do in Your Garage:

1. Store oily, dirty rags near the heater.

2. Don't bother to have a fire extinguisher (or if you have one, stow it under 500 pounds of used tires in the back of the garage).

3. Keep all of your flammable liquids, antifreeze, and other poisonous liquids in soda bottles in an unlocked, open shelf on the floor.

The ideal storage for small items such as nail jars, engine oil, and small cans is on shelves in the area between the studs. These vertical studs are spaced 16 or 24 inches apart, center to center. You can use adjustable tracks and brackets, L braces, individual brackets, or continuous brackets attached to studs to hold up shelves. If your garage walls are made of brick or concrete block, rest freestanding shelves against the walls, or use special masonry fasteners.

TOOLBOX

If you're the sort of person who loves toys, then you may have your eye on one of those big tall red mechanic's toolboxes. They're the ones the professionals use, and they keep everything handy, tidy, and beautifully organized. But like everything else in the car world, you get what you pay for, and all that organization doesn't come cheap. You can spend thousands of dollars on a fancy toolbox and end up with a toolbox that's worth more than your car itself. How much are you really going to use it, anyway?

If you're looking for a less expensive alternative, get a plastic box (they come in all sizes); this way, your tools won't rust, and they'll stay right where you need them. Or buy a small toolbox with drawers that will sit right on your bench.

In addition, consider getting a wrench rack to store individually sized wrenches (you can use it in a drawer or hang it on the wall). Also get some drawer dividers so you can keep sockets separate.

YOU'LL THANK YOURSELF LATER

Power tools and garage lighting should be on different circuits. Install as many circuits as possible to prevent an overload. Several grounded (three-prong) electrical outlets are a necessity, and continuous power strips are a great convenience.

PUTTING IT ALL AWAY

Now that you've got the garage cleaned and some storage units ready to go, you're ready to think about what to do with the tools you have:

- Use all available space, leaving minimum clearances next to, behind, and above vehicles

- Locate all tools, clean them, and then oil them with vegetable oil

- Group items that go together (oil changing supplies, for example)

- Fix any of the tools that were giving you problems

- If you can't repair the tools, then make up a shopping list and replace them

- Find anything that you may need in a pinch (such as a small snow shovel or a fire extinguisher) and store it in an accessible place

QUICK ⓝ PAINLESS

Sliding doors, roll-down window shades, or tilt-out bins make areas more accessible in tight places.

Getting Time on Your Side

	The Old Way	The Lazy Way
Finding a tool	30 minutes	1 minute
Cleaning the garage	5 hours	30 minutes
Working on your car	2 hours	1 hour
Finding the snow shovel during a freak April blizzard	Not until spring thaw	2 seconds
Figuring out whether the tool in your hand is metric or American	Days	A moment
Locating the fire extinguisher in case of emergency	What extinguisher?	1 minute

Even Mario Andretti Does It: Shortcuts and Tips

The secret of saving time while taking care of your car lies in learning all the tips and secrets the pros use. The more shortcuts you make use of, the sooner you'll be *on* the road instead of *beside* it.

WINTERIZING TIPS

There are lots of shortcuts you can take advantage of when trying to save time and effort during the winter months:

- When you're driving in the wintertime, add four 3-tab asphalt roofing shingles to your emergency stash in the trunk. If you get stuck in the snow, you can put a shingle under the wheels for up to six feet of traction.

- If you live in a cold area, get an engine block heater or a lower radiator hose heater controlled by thermostat; it

Spraying WD-40 into your trunk and door lock cylinders may help to prevent freezing. Try it this winter and see!

directly heats the engine coolant and is easy to install.

- Use a dipstick heater for really cold days; just install in place of the regular dipstick (you can use it on more than one car). It will help keep the oil warm.

- Run your air conditioner occasionally in the winter. It will keep the seal lubricated on the air conditioning compressor.

- To heat your motor oil in cold weather, mount a magnetic heater on the steel oil pan. Thermostatically controlled and fairly efficient, these heaters can be used on more than one car, as long as they all have steel pans.

- If you hate to warm up your car on cold days, think about getting an electric blanket for your battery. These battery heaters sell for less than $30 and fit under or around the battery, keeping it warm.

- Lock frozen? If you're at home, plug in your hair dryer and aim at the lock.

- Lock de-icers are handy to thaw a frozen lock, but don't keep yours in the glove compartment where you won't be able to get to it when you need it!

- If you don't have a hair dryer or a de-icer, you can thaw your lock by warming a key with a match or lighter. Hold the key with gloves, and as soon as it's warm, stick it into the lock. You may need to do this several times.

- Driving in temperatures between 25 and 30 degrees Fahrenheit is more dangerous than driving in colder weather because you'll only get half as much traction in wet snow than you would on solidly frozen surfaces at lower temperatures.

- Don't lower the air pressure in tires for better traction in the winter. For every 10 degree drop in temperature, your tire pressure already drops a pound; if you lower it more, your tire will be too low.

- Remember that stopping in snow can take up to four times as long. When the road is slippery, apply the brakes by tapping gently once or twice a second.

- Don't use overdrive in snowy weather; keep the transmission in low gears for better control.

- Keep extra windshield wiper fluid in your trunk during the winter. You can go through quite a lot of fluid trying to keep the muck and slush off your windshield.

MAINTENANCE TIPS

- If your car is under a manufacturer's warranty, let the dealer do any necessary work. You might not be reimbursed for work that you or a local garage perform.

- Extended warranties aren't usually worth the money and usually carry so many exclusions that it's hard to get your money's worth.

QUICK n' PAINLESS

After you wash your car in the winter, treat your door weather stripping with Armor All or a similar product to help keep doors from sticking.

Before starting a repair job, make sure you have all the parts and tools you need on hand. Be sure you've read your manual and understand all the procedures you'll need to do.

- Clean debris that may have accumulated in the radiator or air conditioning condenser occasionally with a garden hose from back to front to force dirt out. Be careful not to bend the fins.

- For information that describes particular problems your car may be having, you can get a technical service bulletin (TSB) online. You'll find a list at http://www.cartalk.com.

- If you turn on your windshield washers and find the water is spraying over the top of your car and splashing on the car behind you, adjust the spray nozzles so the fluid actually hits your windshield.

- If your windshield washers aren't squirting, you may have a clogged nozzle. Clear the nozzle with a pin, needle, or fine wire or flush it with a spray lubricant.

- Use pneumatic and electric tools only to loosen threaded parts and fasteners; never use them to tighten fasteners.

- Keep an unwaxed paper cup on hand when you need to add coolant or windshield wiper fluid to those little compartments. Make a hole in the bottom of the cup and pour the fluid from the jug into the cup into the reservoir. (Or keep a funnel on hand that you use only for this purpose.)

- No matter what type of antifreeze you use, the water/antifreeze mixture is always the same—50/50, unless you encounter temperatures below -34 degrees Fahrenheit (then add more antifreeze). If in doubt, check the chart on the container.

- Always let the engine cool down before replacing your spark plugs.
- Never overfill the transmission; it will lead to air bubbles that won't help lubrication.

Tool Tips

You'll save lots of time with these handy tips:

- To keep all your sockets neat and orderly in their case, glue a thin piece of foam to the lid.
- If you want a good grip on your screwdriver, place a rubber chair leg tip over the handle.

Part Tips

When it comes to parts, you'll find these suggestions can help you do the job faster and easier:

- Newer gas caps have a pressure-vacuum relief valve that is designed to fit a specific car. If you lose a gas cap, be sure to get the right type from an auto parts dealer.
- When you go parts shopping, it's a good idea to have the serial number of your car, the engine number, and the build date. Your owner's manual will tell you where to find these important numbers. Having this information with you can save you a trip back home!
- Don't reuse worn or deformed fasteners; many fasteners are designed to be used only once and may fail if used again. This includes nuts, bolts, washers, self-locking nuts or bolts, and cotter pins.

QUICK n' PAINLESS

Make yourself a cheat sheet to keep in your wallet with your car's vital statistics and never come home with the wrong part again!

SAFETY/COMFORT TIPS

Safety is just as important when you're working under the car as when you're riding inside it. Keep these tips in mind as you work:

- If you hate getting shocked as you slide across the upholstery, keep your hand on the metal door until after you've touched the ground with your foot.

- Long jumper cables are best (at least 12 feet; 16 is better) because they allow you to jump a battery without being nose to nose to another car (such as when you're beside a major highway).

- The best jumper cables are heavier four- or six-gauge wire.

- Store your car's fire extinguisher in the trunk out of direct sunlight, and mount it securely so it doesn't roll around.

- Check your car's fire extinguisher pressure every month.

- Hide an extra key in a magnetic key holder hidden somewhere on your car.

- Tie long hair behind you when you work on your car.

- Light your work area safely with a portable safety light for working inside or under the car. Make sure the bulb is inside a wire cage, and make sure it's a fluorescent bulb (it's safer than an incandescent bulb).

- Wipe up spills immediately, but don't store the oily rags in the garage (they can ignite and burn spontaneously).

- Wear goggles when you operate machine tools or work with battery acid.

- Wear gloves when working with harmful substances.

- Disconnect the negative (-) battery terminal whenever you work on the fuel system or the electrical system. (Beware of computer cautions if you do this.)

- Keep a fire extinguisher handy in your garage.

- Because batteries give off explosive hydrogen gas when charging, keep sparks, lighted matches, and open flames away from the top of the battery. Otherwise, the battery can explode.

- To prevent sparks, connect and disconnect battery cables, jumper cables, or a battery charger only with the ignition off.

- Don't disconnect the battery while the engine is running.

- Don't expose any part of the air conditioning system to high temperatures, which could cause the system to burst.

- Never try to remove or work on your airbags.

- Be careful when using aerosol tire inflators; some are highly flammable.

- Some repairs are beyond your ability. If you don't have the skills or tools to do the job, leave these repairs to the experts.

Congratulations! You've become a safety-minded person. Now treat yourself to a pizza and let someone else do the cooking!

The Lazy Way

- Never work under a car that is running.

- On cars with airbags, never put any stickers or other covering on the steering wheel.

- Don't let chemical cleaners, oil, or grease touch the vinyl covering of the airbag unit.

- When riding in a car with airbags, never hold anything in your hands while the car is moving (objects between you and the airbag can cause injury).

- Before you drain the crankcase, find out what you're going to do with the drained oil.

- Never pour oil onto the ground, down a drain, or into a stream, pond, or lake.

- Many types of grease, lubricants, and other chemicals can be absorbed directly through the skin. Read warnings carefully and avoid skin contact.

- Don't service your air-conditioning system unless you're a well-trained mechanic. The refrigerant is extremely cold when compressed, and when released into the air will instantly freeze anything it contacts—including your eyes. The refrigerant becomes a deadly poisonous gas in the presence of an open flame, and one good whiff of vapors from burning refrigerant can be fatal.

CLEANING TIPS

Cleaning your car needn't take up an entire weekend. Follow these suggestions and you'll be back on the sofa in front of the TV in no time:

- If water beads up on your windshield and won't wipe away, you've got air-pollution problems. Try using stronger solvents on the windshield (such as a wax remover), but watch out for the car's paint.

- Windshield smears are caused by worn blades, an incorrect mixture of cleaner/solvent, or a dirty windshield or wiper.

- If your wipers smear in just one direction, that's probably because it's very cold outside or old age has hardened your wiper blades.

- Replace wiper blades every six months for the best view.

- If your car is covered with dried sap, try pushing it off with a plastic spatula.

- Don't wipe down a car that's been in the rain; all kinds of grit are in the water on the car. Wiping down the car at this time will scratch the finish.

- To protect your car's finish, keep your car in a garage, out of the sun, and away from airborne corrosives. If you can't garage it, keep it under a carport or under a car cover.

- Hose off your car often when it's covered with dirt and grime.

- If you can't stick your vacuum into those little cracks in the car, poke a plastic straw through the bottom of a stiff paper cup and put some caulk around the straw. Put the cup into the end of the vacuum; the suction will hold it in place.

IF YOU'RE SO
INCLINED

Cover your car when it has to sit out in the elements and protect your finish!

Getting Time On Your Side

	The Old Way	The Lazy Way
Winterizing your car	Could be hours	30 minutes
Cleaning your car	Could be days	20 minutes
Protecting your car while you work on it	Oops!	2 seconds
Maintaining your tools	Not until it's too late	30 minutes and now you're ahead of the game!
Finding the part you need	5 trips	1 trip
Staying safe while you work on your car	Uh-oh	5 seconds

Chapter five

Zooming Down the Backstretch: Follow-Up Tips

You don't have time to wait for the tow truck, the auto club, or your friend Sal to come bail you out when you've been too busy to keep gas in the tank, check the oil, or make sure the fan belts don't fly off. The simple truth is, the easiest way to make owning a car an effortless experience is to do your own preventive maintenance. This chapter explains how.

EVERY OTHER FILL-UP

It may seem like overkill, but especially if you have an older car, you'll thank yourself for doing this:

- Check oil; add oil if necessary. (See chapter 6.)

QUICK **n** PAINLESS

Just a few minutes here
and there doing simple
checks will save you
oodles of time and money
later...it's worth it!

WEEKLY

Once a week, whether you think you need it or not, run
through this quickie car check:

- Check the antifreeze level (if you're lucky, your car
  will have a transparent reservoir with level mark-
  ings). If you're low, fill the antifreeze reservoir with
  a 50/50 solution of water and antifreeze.

- Check the windshield wiper fluid; be sure there is
  enough antifreeze in fluid during the winter.

- Clean your windshield and inspect your wiper
  blades. Don't wait until the rubber is dried and brittle to replace them.

- Check tire pressure.

- Look for cuts, bulges, or excessive wear in the tires.

- If a tire is significantly low, check for leaks. (See
  Chapter 6.)

MONTHLY

These checks only take a few minutes once a month, and
you'll be glad you did them the first time you uncover a
problem:

- Inspect your belts and hoses. Tighten them when
  they are slack by more than a half-inch. Replace rotten, bulging, or brittle hoses. (If your hose looks
  funny or feels too soft or hard, replace it.)

- Check clamps. Tighten them if necessary.

- Replace worn, glazed, or frayed belts.

- Check automatic transmission fluid with the engine warm and running and the parking brake on. (See Chapter 12.)

- Check the brake fluid. (See Chapter 10.)

- Check the power steering fluid. (See Chapter 14.)

EVERY OTHER MONTH

This isn't something you need to do often, but don't forget to:

- Check the air filter.

EVERY 3 MONTHS OR 3,000 MILES

Regardless of how well you've been keeping up with your weekly and monthly checks, make sure to check all the elements listed below every 3 months or 3,000 miles. You'll thank yourself later!

- Change oil. (See Chapter 6.)

- Check breather element.

- Check PCV filter.

- Check battery. (See Chapter 6.)

- Check manual transmission fluid levels. (See Chapter 12.)

- Check differential fluid levels.

- Rotate tires.

YOU'LL THANK YOURSELF LATER

Don't forget that air filter! Your engine is at its best when air is circulating through it properly!

ONCE A YEAR OR EVERY 15,000 MILES

Pick a regular time of year to do these jobs, and you won't forget: the beginning of a season is nice...

- Replace your wiper blades at least once a year, if you haven't done so before. You should check them each time you clean your windshield.
- Change automatic transmission fluid and filter. (See Chapter 12.)
- Flush cooling system.
- Get safety and/or emissions inspections (required in some states).
- Replace air filter. (See Chapter 9.)
- Replace PCV filter. (See Chapter 13.)
- Change charcoal canister.
- Check timing belt condition.

EVERY TWO YEARS

You don't need to do this often, but don't forget to:

- Flush brake fluid.

KEEP TRACK OF YOUR CAR MAINTENANCE

Write the date or miles by each item when you replace or change it:

- ☐ Air cleaner
- ☐ Air filter

YOU'LL THANK YOURSELF LATER

It's especially important to check the differential fluid level if you notice any leaks or seepage. To find out how to check these levels, read your owner's manual.

- [ ] Automatic transmission filter
- [ ] Automatic transmission fluid
- [ ] Battery
- [ ] Belts
- [ ] Brake checks
- [ ] Brake fluid
- [ ] Carburetor
- [ ] Chassis lubrication
- [ ] Coolant
- [ ] Cooling system flush
- [ ] Fuel filter
- [ ] Oil filter
- [ ] PCV valve
- [ ] Power steering fluid
- [ ] Radiator hose
- [ ] Spark plugs
- [ ] Timing belt
- [ ] Tire check
- [ ] Tire rotation
- [ ] Transmission fluid
- [ ] Wheel bearings
- [ ] Windshield wiper fluid

A COMPLETE WASTE OF TIME

The 3 Worst Things to Do When It Comes to Maintaining Your Car:

1. Don't keep your fluids topped up.

2. Forget to maintain your spare when you maintain your other tires.

3. Ignore warning signs (like cracked belts).

Getting Time On Your Side

	The Old Way	The Lazy Way
Changing the oil	30 minutes	15 minutes
Putting the car in the shop	Every other week	Once every 3 months (for your quarterly tune-up!)
Fixing a flat	Every month or so	Half as often!
Jump-starting the car	Once a month	Never again! (You've been checking your battery regularly!)
Running out of gas in the middle of the highway!	Every few weeks	Never again!
Peering through a grimy windshield	Every time it rains	Never again!

Part 3

Keeping Your Car Running Without Running Yourself Ragged

Are You Too Lazy to Read Keeping Your Car Running Without Running Yourself Ragged?

1 You can tell it's time to add water to your cooling system when you're parked by the side of the road watching Old Faithful erupt from the front of your hood. ☐ yes ☐ no

2 The easiest way to deal with stains on your car's upholstery is to throw a blanket over the seat and forget about it. ☐ yes ☐ no

3 A tune-up is something an orchestra does before beginning a concert. ☐ yes ☐ no

Stop and Go: Maintain Your Car in 60 Minutes a Month

There you are, all dressed up in your best suit and in a hurry to get to work for that big presentation. You slip the key into the ignition only to hear the dreaded sound of a car engine on its last piston. Dimly you remember something about a lube job that never got done, and now it's too late.

If you're like most folks with a car, you expect it to run, but you don't have much time to spend fooling around under the hood. But again if you're like most folks, you dread taking the car in for servicing. Maybe you've watched one too many *60 Minutes* exposés about dishonest repair shops. If you're a woman, maybe you just don't like being called "little lady." Or maybe you don't like spending lots of money for things you figure you ought to be able to do yourself.

Of course, the truly effortless way to maintain your car is to have someone else do it, and that's exactly what I recommend for many complex car jobs. The days of every car owner doubling as a car expert went the way of the Edsel. On the other hand, there are a variety of things you can do to maintain your car that take less time than making an appointment three weeks from now to get your car serviced and waiting around for the car to be done.

The most effortless way to prevent time-consuming car problems is to spend a moment or two up front doing a little preventive maintenance, which means you're fixing it before it breaks. It's the ultimate lazy way, provided you follow the easy steps we're going to present to you. Be sure to follow them all! If you think you don't have time to do the job correctly the first time, you definitely won't have time to do it twice.

ONCE A WEEK WHETHER IT NEEDS IT OR NOT

There are some preventive maintenance jobs you should do every week, so you don't get stranded out on the Serengeti without a viable form of transportation. Most important is the oil level, because a car without oil will freeze up faster than an ice cube in the Antarctic. While you're at it, take a peek at the coolant and windshield washer fluid, and check the tire pressure. (Note: the pressure will be higher just after driving, so check it when the tires are cold.) These jobs don't take long, and you'll be glad you did them.

Dip that Stick

Listen and repeat after us: Check your oil level every week, and replace your oil every 3,000 miles (or 3 months, whichever comes first). If this sounds fairly rigorous, you need to realize just how important clean oil is. After all, would you make salsa every night with your Cuisinart and never clean the equipment? After a few hundred whirls, those blades would get pretty gunky. The same thing can happen to your car's engine if you don't bother to replace the old oil and filter.

When you turn the key and your engine starts running, the oil pump in the lower part of the engine starts pushing oil through passages to lubricate moving parts. After the oil lubes everything up, it flows back down to the crankcase, where it gets sucked up again by the oil pump and passes through the oil filter before the whole process starts over again. With time, as the oil gets circulated over and over, things start to get a bit sticky—sort of like what your arteries would look like after 65 years of downing jelly doughnuts and cream cheese. Sludge—in the form of moisture, acid, gums and resin, dust, dirt, and fine metal particles—starts to build up in the engine.

The way you drive your car affects how much of this sludge accumulates, just like the way you eat affects how much fatty gunk builds up in your arteries. Two people with the exact same car will have different oil needs depending on the way they drive. If Joe drives his car to his office a half block from his home and never takes it anywhere else, you can figure that (a) he's not a lot of yuks at a party, and (b) his engine will look much worse

A COMPLETE WASTE OF TIME

The 3 Worst Things to Do with Used Motor Oil:

1. Pour it down the toilet.
2. Throw it out in the garbage.
3. Bury it in the ground.

than Sue's, who puts 30,000 miles a year on her car in highway driving.

This difference is because fuel doesn't start burning completely until the engine warms up (about seven miles in warm weather, twice that in cold). When fuel doesn't burn completely, it produces more contaminants (such as moisture and acid) that muck up the oil. These contaminants can clog the engine. So if you're strictly a to-church-and-back Sunday driver, you should definitely change your oil every 3,000 miles. If most of your time is spent flying along the freeways for hours at a clip, you could stretch that amount out to 6,000 miles, although most mechanics prefer the 3,000 figure.

Check the Oil Level

1. Park the car on a level spot with the engine off.

2. Open the hood and grab the oil dipstick.

3. Remove the dipstick, wiping it on a paper towel.

4. Reinsert the dipstick all the way into the tube.

5. Again remove the dipstick and check the level; you won't need to add more oil unless you can see the "add" line.

   If you need to add oil, read on!

What Do All Those Numbers Mean?

If you have to add oil, the first thing you need to know is what kind of oil to add. If you've ever wandered into a service station in search of a package of cheese crackers,

QUICK **n** PAINLESS

For utmost accuracy, always check the oil dipstick with the engine off, so the oil has a chance to drain to the bottom pan.

you may have noticed a line of oilcans featuring a virtual alphabet soup of designations on the label.

Oilcans are labeled with a letter code, ranging from SA, SB, SC, SD, SE, SF, CA, CB, CC, and CD. Codes beginning with the letter *S* are intended for normal gas engines; those with a *C* are for diesel engines. The service group that's recommended for your car will be listed in your service manual, but SF is the best grade of engine oil, and SA is the worst. (The scale is open-ended, so if an even better grade of oil comes out, it will be lettered SG.)

Now, suppose you've pulled a can off the shelf that says *SAE 10W-30SF*. The first letters (SAE) refer to the Society of Automotive Engineers, who invented this numbering system, which is why it gets to put its initials on the can. The 10W-30 part refers to the oil's viscosity (thickness). The thinnest oil is a 5, and as you move up to 10, 20, 30 and on up to 90, the oil gets so thick you could stand your morning toast up in it. Basically, 90 motor oil has graduated to grease.

Is 10 Enough? Is 40 Too Many?

So now you know what the can is saying, but how do you know which type to pour into your car? It depends on the weather. Just as you'd use different waxes on your skis for different sorts of snow, your car needs different weights of oil depending on how hot or cold it is. If you're standing in a Maine snowdrift in the middle of winter, you're going to want an oil that is thin enough to be able to lubricate the engine even before it's warmed up. When the engine gets hot, it thins out the oil, so if

Congratulations! You've figured out what all those letters mean on your oil label! Time to go to a drive-in movie!

The Lazy Way

the weather is very hot, you don't want the oil to be so thin that it can't lubricate properly.

In the old days, folks were always having to drain and replace their oil according to the vagaries of the weather. But today's lazy car owners can rejoice and buy multiple viscosity oils; a 10W-30, for example, has a 10 weight in the winter, and a 30-weight in the heat: it's an oil for all seasons.

If you're filling your car with more than one can of oil, you should use all the same kind, but you don't need to worry if you're adding a quart of oil that's different from what is already in there—they're all compatible. If you want to be daring and try a different viscosity of oil, you don't need to drain the old oil first.

The Pressure Is On

It's always a good idea to check the tire pressure with a tire gauge once a week or so. Don't forget the spare! If you leave it slumbering in the trunk under a pile of *National Geographics*, you'll never notice it slowly deflating itself. Then when you're out on the road with a flat on some dark and stormy night, you'll have no one but yourself to blame when you pull out a spare as limp as a piece of leftover fettuccine. Tests by a major tire manufacturer show that 90 percent of all cars have at least one tire that's improperly inflated.

Never exceed the maximum inflation pressure listed on the side of the tire, and keep in mind that this maximum isn't usually the correct pressure for everyday driving. Instead, read your owner's manual (or sticker on the car) to find out the recommended tire pressure for your car.

1. If you have radial tires, don't gauge the correct pressure just by looking. Radial tires have a sidewall bulge that may make them look low when they aren't.

2. Check air pressure when the tires are cold (pressure increases with temperature). If you must move the car to check the pressure, don't drive more than a mile.

3. To check pressure, press the tire gauge straight down so no air escapes.

4. If a tire is low, be sure to fill it during the next service station stop.

While you're checking the tire pressure, check the tread, too. State laws mandate that tires should have at least $1/16$ of an inch to pass inspection, but that's pretty hard to estimate by a quick glance. Instead, grab a Lincoln penny and stick him head first into the most worn part of the tire. If you can still see the top of his head, your tire is too worn, and it won't pass an inspection. If at least some of his head disappears into the rubber, then you're safe.

Now for the Coolant Level

When you check the coolant level and freezing point, you can't just open the radiator cap and see the coolant in there; it all looks like plain water floating around.

YOU'LL THANK YOURSELF LATER

The tire gauge on the end of the air hose at the corner gas station isn't accurate enough because it suffers too much abuse. Carry your own reliable tire pressure gauge.

Instead, you need to use an antifreeze tester, a syringe-like instrument with some colored balls at the top and a long hose at the bottom. If your coolant level is not high enough, you'll need to add more. If the freezing point is not low enough, it's time to change the coolant. (For instructions on adding coolant, see Chapter 16.)

1. Run your engine a few minutes before testing.

2. Carefully remove the radiator cap. (It will be under some pressure.)

3. Insert the antifreeze tester hose into the radiator and suck up some coolant.

4. Count the number of balls that float.

5. Read the chart on the tester to figure out the temperature at which your coolant is protected.

Checking Washer Solvent

If you've ever driven down a wintry country road peering through a thick coating of oatmeal-like sludge on your windshield, you've come to appreciate the cleaning capability of your windshield washing solvent. If you don't have much time to maintain your car, you certainly won't have the time to stop every few miles to wipe off your windshield, so once a week, be sure to check your solvent reservoir. It's also a good idea to carry an extra jug of solvent along with you so you can add some if you encounter a particularly messy ride.

If you're mechanically challenged and you're pretty sure you wouldn't be able to recognize the solvent

Congratulations! You've kept your washer fluid topped up and made it home safely during that last storm! Relax with a good book and a cup of hot chocolate!

The Lazy Way

reservoir if it sat up and bit you, get out your owner's manual and look it up. There will be a diagram that you can follow. If you're a more daring sort, throw the manual aside and try this on your own:

1. Open the hood and locate the reservoir.

2. Lift the cap and pour in the washer solvent until the reservoir is three-quarters full.

THE EVERY-THREE-MONTHS COMPLETE MAINTENANCE CHECK

The best time to do an overall maintenance check is at the same time you perform your oil change, which normally should be about every 3,000 miles or 3 months. As long as you're messing about in there with the oil, you might as well take stock of the rest of the car.

Here's what to check:

- Battery fluid levels (unless you have a maintenance-free, lazy battery)
- Automatic transmission fluid level
- Power steering fluid level
- Manual transmission and differential fluid levels
- Drive belts (V belt, Serpentine belt)
- Lights
- Electrical accessories
- Wiper blades
- Spare tire

IF YOU'RE SO INCLINED

While you're filling your washer solvent reservoir, pour a bit of solvent onto a clean cloth and clean your wiper blades. Your wipers will work better and last longer.

A COMPLETE WASTE OF TIME

The 3 Worst Things You Can Do when Working on Your Car:

1. Support a car on cinder blocks or other props that might crumble.

2. Work on a car supported only by a jack.

3. Work under a car while the engine is running.

After you've checked everything, take this opportunity to rotate your tires.

Change Is Good

It's been 3,000 miles, and now you're ready to change the oil and oil filter. Before you begin, gather up all your equipment so that you can spend as little time as possible on this job. Organization is the key to *The Lazy Way!*

Changing the Oil

Here's what you'll need to do an oil change:

Car jack/stands

Owner's manual

Tool for oil drain plug (a socket)

Container for old oil

Oil filter tool

New oil filter

New oil (usually four to five quarts, but check your manual)

1 Because warm oil drains more completely, run the engine for a few minutes first.

2 Park the car on a flat surface and turn off the engine.

3 Block the car's wheels to keep the car from rolling.

4 Jack up the car and follow all safety precautions.

5 Identify the engine oil plug (you'll usually find it in the center of the engine oil pan).

6 Remove the plug with your socket and drain the old oil into the container.

7 Replace the plug, tightening it with your hand before using the socket.

8 Remove the old oil filter with the oil filter tool.

9 Pour oil in the center hole of the filter until it saturates the element. (This way, your engine gets oil as soon as you start the car).

10 Smear a film of clean oil on the filter sealing gasket.

11 Install the filter, being careful not to damage the rubber seal on the filter as you replace it. Hand tighten the filter to the specifications on the filter, but be careful; if you start the thing off crooked, you can damage the seal and cause a leak.

12 Pour the new oil into the opening on the valve cover.

13 With the car off the jack, start the engine to circulate the oil; turn off the engine and check oil level.

14 Note the mileage and date. It's a good idea to put a sticker on a corner of your windshield noting the next due date or mileage to check the oil.

15 Properly dispose of the old oil.

Batteries

Newer cars have maintenance-free batteries, so if you lazy car owners have wised up and gotten one of those,

QUICK 🆖 **PAINLESS**

Catch drained oil in suitable containers. Don't use beverage containers—that might mislead someone into drinking from them.

To clean up fresh oil spills on your garage floor, pour some cat litter on the spot. When the litter has absorbed the oil, grab a broom and sweep away the mess. Unless you want a big mess, use traditional clay litter, not the clumping variety.

you can skip this section. For the rest of you with older cars, you'll need to add water to your battery at regular intervals. (If the water gets too low, the battery won't hold a charge.) Take off the caps from each of the six cells of the battery and check the water level (it should be up to the rings). If it's not, add more, using regular tap water (you don't need to distill the water first anymore). Be very careful when you add the water because the battery contains acid that could splash out as you top off the fluids.

Power Steering Reservoir

On most models, the power steering reservoir is marked on the cap. Remove the lid, and check the level using the handy dipstick attached to the cap. Add more if needed. (See Chapter 14 for details.)

Rotate Those Tires

Unless you want to limp around on uneven tires that are wearing out at different rates, it's a good idea to rotate your tires at every oil change. There are several methods for tire rotation; you can use the method recommended in your owner's manual, or you can use this one:

1. Move the front tires straight back, with the right front to right rear and left front to left rear.

2. Move the back tires to the front.

If you have a full-sized spare, let it join in the rotational fun. Check your manual for the precise method to perform a five-tire rotation that's designed for your type of car.

Belts

Every time you change the oil, check the belts to make sure there aren't any cracks, frays, or dry spots that could signal a problem. If the belts are loose, adjust them. If the cracks are getting deep, replace the belts as soon as possible. While you're at it, check over your owner's manual for recommendations on when to change the belts.

Important: Don't forget the replacement interval recommended for the timing belt, if your car has one. The timing belt may be out of sight under a cover or shield and could cause serious damage if broken.

Lights Out!

You'd be surprised how many people are driving around in the dark with a burned-out brake light or interior light—or even a missing front light—and wondering why they can't see where they're going. In order to stay one step ahead of the law (it's illegal to drive around without functioning exterior lights), check all lights at every oil change.

Check brake lights, turn signals, interior lights, the overhead light, and the trunk light. Replace any bulbs that are burned out. If a new bulb doesn't solve the problem, you could have a bad switch or electrical ground, which means it's time for a trip to your mechanic.

Shine the headlights on your garage door to check whether the lights are level. If they're not level, take the car to the repair shop for adjustment.

IF YOU'RE SO INCLINED

If possible, install radial tires. You'll get up to a half-mile more per gallon than you would with bias-belted tires.

Getting Time on Your Side

	The Old Way	The Lazy Way
Changing oil	With every weather change	Every 3 months
Adding battery water	Every 3,000 miles	Never again!
Cleaning up oil spills	30 minutes	5 minutes
Changing the oil filter	30 minutes	10 minutes
Keeping your wipers clean	Only by replacing them	2 seconds
Disposing of old oil	Maybe never	10 minutes

Looking Good: Car Cosmetics

Even the laziest car owner wants to keep the car looking spiffy—as long as it's not too hard to do. How we feel about our car dictates how we treat it. A vehicle that is clean inside and out is usually not driven as hard and is mechanically in much better shape.

WINDSHIELDS

One of the most important places to start when you're thinking about cleaning the car is the windshield, because trying to drive with dirty glass is a safety hazard. A clean windshield also improves your night vision.

When you're cleaning your windshield, remember to clean both sides of the glass, and don't forget to clean the headlights while you're at it. Use an aerosol type of automotive glass cleaner; the foam stays put and does a better job than household glass cleaner.

When you're cleaning the windshield, use crumpled newspaper to clean and dry the glass without streaking. Or you can use a windshield sponge/squeegee like the gas station attendants use. Keep one in a bucket filled with windshield washer solution stored in your garage, for washing the windows and headlights in between gas station visits.

Erasing Windshield Scratches

A scratch in your windshield can be distracting and annoying, but there are ways to deal with it without having to replace the entire windshield. You should repair any chips or bull's-eyes immediately. If you don't, most windshields will develop cracks, and you'll have to replace the entire windshield—and who has time for that?

1. Put a bit of jeweler's rouge on a cloth and rub over the scratch and then wash off the residue. (You can buy this stuff from a jewelry store or glass shop.)

2. If that doesn't work, stop by an auto glass shop and find out whether they can remove it with a commercial polishing agent. However, if the scratch is so deep you can feel it with your fingers, odds are it can't be rubbed out.

3. A glass repair shop can probably repair even a stone chip in your windshield if it's smaller than a quarter, has no jagged edges, and isn't in front of the driver. Expect to pay between $50 and $150. Some insurance companies will pay the deductible to have this

repaired, because they realize it's cheaper to do that than replace the entire windshield at $500. You may want to contact your insurance company to verify that they'll pay the deductible.

KEEPING IT CLEAN

If you want to protect your car's finish, you've got to give it a bath now and then. But most people do it all wrong, starting with the dish detergent they use for soap. Household detergents are much too harsh for car finishes, stripping off the wax and drying the paint itself.

Next, most people like to wash the car on a nice, sunny day, because they're going to get all sloppy and wet. But washing your car in direct sun will guarantee a spotty surface, and cold water on a hot car finish can leave tiny little cracks in the finish.

Washing the Car

Here's what you need to wash your car the right way:

- Automotive wheel cleaner
- Automotive car wash
- Soft brush or sponge
- Automotive wax and polish
- Chamois
- Bucket

1 Make sure your car is cool, and park it in the shade if it's a sunny day.

QUICK ⬛ PAINLESS

Unfold a portable sunscreen across the inside of your windshield on hot, sunny days. You'll protect your dashboard and help keep it from cracking.

2 Choose a car wash product specially formulated not to harm the finish.

3 Begin with the wheels and tires first, using the special tire/wheel cleaners.

4 Flush the bucket to remove dirty water, and then fill it with cool water and car wash soap.

5 Rinse the car first to remove dirt.

6 Soap it with a clean, soft brush, sponge, or cloth.

7 Rinse off the soap.

8 Dry the car with a clean towel or chamois.

9 If you have a convertible, apply a vinyl protectant to the top after each wash. The protectant restores the shine and extends the top's life. Don't scrub the soft plastic rear window; just flush it with fresh water.

WAXING POETIC

We know, you don't have lots of time to waste putzing around with waxing your car. But a good wax can protect your car's finish, which is under constant attack from the environment. A good wax job before winter can protect it from snow, salt, and ice. When summer comes, another heavy wax coat can protect the car from the sun. In fact, it's more important to protect your car from the sun than from winter's salt and ice. A little time now will pay big dividends later on.

YOU'LL THANK YOURSELF LATER

Don't use too much car wash soap, or it will be too hard to rinse off and will leave a hazy film.

Choose a wax depending on the kind of car you have:

- New car: use a polysealer or nonabrasive pure wax for clearcoat finishes
- Year-old car: use a cleaner/wax to strip old wax, remove road film, and clean the paint surface; most cleaner/waxes work on clearcoat finishes
- A car with a dull, weathered finish: use a finish restorer or polishing/rubbing compound

You can start waxing the car after you've washed and dried it. Of course, you'll read the instructions on the wax first, but here are the general rules for waxing your car *The Lazy Way:*

1. Dampen a cloth or old T-shirt and apply a light, even coat of wax to a small section of the car.

2. Immediately buff the car with an electric buffer—it takes much less effort than buffing with a cotton diaper. Don't put on too much pressure or pause while buffing, or the buffer can burn the paint or scratch the surface of the car.

REPAIRING PAINT NICKS AND CHIPS

Your car accumulates and is exposed to numerous particles that will hurt its paint job, such as pollutants, mud, salt, sand, bugs, tar, rain, snow, sun. If you've got a newer car, your paint job is rust-resistant, but older cars run the risk of major rust problems when their paint chips. If you notice some dings in your car's paint job after the time

A COMPLETE WASTE OF TIME

The 3 Worst Things You Can Do with Car Wax:

1. Put it on and forget it until it's baked into the finish.

2. Use an abrasive wax on a clearcoat finish.

3. Apply wax on a hot car in direct sunlight.

that lady ran her grocery cart into your Saab, reach for a small vial of replacement paint—you can buy it from your dealer or an auto parts store. Select one that matches your car's finish and follow the instructions on the package. If you find the little brush that comes with the paint kit too annoying, take a match out of a book and use the torn end as a brush.

SPRUCING UP THE UPHOLSTERY

Chowing down on a Big Mac as you're tooling down the freeway may seem like a good idea, until you dribble Special Sauce all over the upholstery. When the fabric gets stained, you should act fast before the stain sets and ruins the look (or smell!) of your interior. You can buy special car upholstery cleaner, but any household carpet or fabric cleaner works just as well. However, if your car has leather or vinyl seats, you need to buy an approved cleaner from an auto parts store.

Cleaning the Upholstery

To clean your upholstery, you'll need:

> Towel
> Scrub brush
> Carpet cleaner/fabric cleaner or detergent
> Water

1 Spray on the fabric cleaner. Let stand for period of time (as specified on can).

2 Allow the upholstery to air dry.

3 Scrub with scrub brush.

4 Dry area, feathering edges with towel to eliminate streaks.

Repairing a Tear

When you spot a small tear in your vinyl seat, act quickly before the tear turns into the Grand Canyon and splits the seat in two. Here's what you'll need:

Masking tape

Razor knife/scissors

Glue applicators (thin straws or matches)

Good quality plastic or vinyl cement

1 Pull the torn edges together and tape the tear shut with masking tape, leaving small gaps.

2 Put only a drop or two of cement on the match or straw, and slide it along the length of the tear, spreading the cement evenly. Don't glue over the masking tape, and make sure the edges of the tear are perfectly aligned. It's better to use too little cement than too much. If you take your time, the repair will be almost unnoticeable.

3 Let the glue dry overnight and then carefully remove the tape.

DECAL/STICKER REMOVAL

You bought a used car from a Deadhead, and now you're just dying to remove that Grateful Dead decal and the

Congratulations! You've scrubbed your upholstery until the nubs shine. Now go get another Big Mac, but eat this one in the restaurant!

The Lazy Way

Flower Power symbol in the rear window. You'll be glad to hear that it's not as hard as it looks.

First try spraying on some lubricant before peeling off. If that doesn't work, hold a hair dryer close to soften the adhesive; then peel the decal off. Dealer emblems are more stubborn, but they may give way to prying with a rubber spatula or a wide putty knife (cover the blade with duct tape first). Heat the area with a hair dryer and then wiggle your utensil under the emblem.

Once you've got the decal off, go over any remaining adhesive with a cloth dampened with rubbing alcohol. If there are some really stubborn areas, scrape them with a fingernail. The alcohol will remove the adhesive, but it will also remove wax, so buff the area with a polishing compound and then apply a fresh coat of wax.

RESTORING FADED PAINT

If your car looks faded and dull right after you washed it, your paint job has probably oxidized. Blame the hot sun and road grit, but if you run your finger along the paint and no color rubs off, relax! You've been spared a new paint job. You can restore the finish *The Lazy Way,* with an abrasive polish.

1. With a clean cloth diaper, buff a small area with a mildly abrasive cleaner or polish.

2. If you like the way that looks, keep going.

3. Areas that are really dull (like your roof) may need a more abrasive polish. But be careful not to take off too much paint.

YOU'LL THANK YOURSELF LATER

It's better to polish often than to use an occasional hand-rubbing compound (it's easier on the finish). From least to most abrasive polishes, the available polish types are:

- Liquid cleaner/polish

- Paste polishing compounds

- Paste hand-rubbing compounds

4. When the shine is back, apply just one coat of a
   good paste wax to protect the paint.

BLACK THOSE TIRES!

To keep your tires healthy, apply a tire dressing and protectant so they can withstand sun, salt, and chemicals.
This will extend the length of your tires, which is a major
element to keeping yourself and your loved ones safe.

QUICK ⬛ *PAINLESS*

Watch out for those finish
restorer ads that claim to
revitalize your faded paint
with a tinted product.
These products can actu-
ally discolor your paint job.

Getting Time on Your Side

	The Old Way	The Lazy Way
Cleaning the windshield	20 minutes	5 minutes
Defogging windows	10 minutes	1 minute
Repairing windshield scratches	1 hour	20 minutes
Protecting the dash	1 hour	2 seconds
Buffing car wax	3 hours	1 hour
Cleaning upholstery	An afternoon	1 hour

The Doctor Is In: 60-Second Diagnosis of Clinks, Smells, and Leaks

You're driving down the highway minding your own business when suddenly you hear CLINK! CLINK! CLINK! CLINK! CLINK! CLINK! If you're like most folks, you turn up the radio and keep on driving. Who's got time to drive to the repair shop and try to explain the noise (which of course won't appear when the mechanic drives your car)?

Just as your body typically warns you of an impending stroke or heart attack, so your car uses these little noises to let you know that something is rotten in Denmark. When your car starts making a funny noise, emitting a strange smell, or leaking fluid, there's a reason. Figuring out what that reason is could save you lots of time and money down the road.

A COMPLETE WASTE OF TIME

The 3 Worst Things to Do when You Hear or Smell Something Odd in Your Car:

1. Wait a month to see if it goes away.

2. Turn up the radio or open the car windows.

3. Figure it's normal aging and ignore it.

NOISES 101

Most of the time, when your car starts making a weird sound, it's an indication that you need to take your car in for a repair. You'll help your mechanic if you can answer a few basic questions in addition to mimicking the noise:

- Do you hear the noise when the car is idling, moving, or both?

- Does the sound change when you speed up or slow down?

- Do you hear the noise on a bumpy road or a smooth straight stretch?

- Is the noise louder when the car is cold or hot?

- Do you hear this noise only in reverse, forward, or on right or left turns (or both)?

Backfire

If you're driving down the road and you hear someone firing a pistol in your ear, relax! It's probably not a carjacker, but your car backfiring. This sound occurs when a spark plug fires while a valve is open. An engine that backfires needs immediate attention from an expert, however. A backfire through the carburetor can ignite, and a backfire through the exhaust system can put a hole in the muffler.

Bang

A steady banging under the hood is an emergency; turn off the car right away. This sound could mean that the engine has a damaged rod bearing or a failing connecting rod. You'll have to pay big bucks if a connecting rod knocks a hole through the engine wall.

Clack

No, it's not your mom running up some curtains on her old Singer; it's probably a noise coming from the valve lifters at the lower part of the engine or the rocker arms at the top. If you're sluggish about changing your oil, you may hear these clacking noises. If the noise is soft or goes away after you start the car, you can probably live with it. But a sudden loud clacking sound needs to be checked by a mechanic, or you risk an expensive valve job.

Click

If your car clicks whenever you round a sharp curve, you probably have a worn CV joint that needs to be repaired quickly. This noise won't go away and will continue to worsen until the joint breaks.

Clunk

That loud *clunk!* you hear when you step on the gas could well be the sound of your engine dropping into place. The cause of this sound is a broken engine mount; when you accelerate under these conditions, the engine actually flies up in the air. This broken mount needs to be fixed at the repair shop. If you hear the clunk when you put the car into gear, it means there's some slack in the drive line, which usually is a problem that you don't need to worry about right away.

QUICK **n** PAINLESS

Identify any sounds you hear your car making as soon as you can, and you'll save yourself from getting stuck in the middle of the road later on!

Grinding

Nothing is more excruciatingly painful to listen to than metal on metal, which is what you're hearing if your brakes grind when you apply them. The cause is probably a badly worn brake lining, which means you should head to the nearest repair shop without passing *Go*. It's also possible for the transmission to make this sound, but don't worry about which problem it is—either way, you need a mechanic's help.

Groan

If you have trouble turning the wheel and hear a groan or growl that sounds like something from a Stephen King novel, you may have low power steering fluid. The noise will stop if you add more fluid, but you need to find out why the stuff is leaking out in the first place. Ask your mechanic at the first opportunity.

Hiss

Unless you're driving around with a python in the back seat, this noise is usually caused by a leaking vacuum hose as you idle. If the car starts idling roughly or heavily, the vacuum hose is broken or has come off its port. You can fix this sound yourself.

1. Look under the hood and see if you can locate the origin of the hiss.

2. If you can, turn off the engine and check for a broken or moved vacuum hose. If the hose is just dislodged, pop it back where it belongs.

Congratulations! You've figured out what that weird sound really means to your car! Take a break and watch a favorite movie!

The Lazy Way

3. If you don't feel comfortable replacing the broken hose, get your car to the repair shop because a broken hose will cause a rough-running engine.

Knock/Ping

If your car pings and knocks when you speed up, you've got an engine combustion problem. Low octane gas may cause pinging. The simple solution is to fill up with high-octane fuel the next time you go to the gas station and see whether the noise goes away. If it doesn't, you need to see your mechanic, because long-term pinging can lead to engine wear.

Rattle

We don't mean that annoying sound you get when your son's marbles are rolling around on the dashboard—this noise occurs outside the car, often in the rear. It may be the result of loose exhaust parts, although bumper guards can also make this sound. Rattles aren't usually too hard to find or fix.

Roar

If you've ever cringed behind the wheel because your mild-mannered car suddenly erupts like a squad of Hells' Angels, your car probably has an exhaust system problem. The roaring noise will get worse when you speed up, and it could be the result of a hole either in the muffler or exhaust pipes. This problem won't hurt your car, but besides sounding awful, it can poison you if carbon monoxide from the exhaust leaks into the car.

IF YOU'RE SO
INCLINED

Use the fuel with the right octane rating for your car (look in the manual). A higher rating is a waste of money, and a lower rating won't give good performance.

You could get a ticket for driving a car that violates local noise pollution limits, so have a noisy muffler fixed ASAP.

Singing

No, we don't mean like something from the Vienna Boys' Choir. Singing sounds come in a whole variety of pitches, and they are usually caused by worn-out bearings:

- High pitch: the ailing bearing is probably in your air conditioner, alternator, transmission, or heater blower motor
- Variable pitch: wheel bearings (noise may change when you turn right or left)
- Humming: rear-end bearings (noise changes when you slow down and speed up, usually on a smooth road)

Squeak

Some cars always squeak when you apply the brakes, and if yours does this, don't worry. But if your car develops a new squeak when you stomp on the brake, the brake-wear sensor may have detected a problem. Get the sound checked by your mechanic.

If your car squeaks when you drive on a bumpy road, your steering or suspension parts may need to be lubricated. If the squeak is rhythmic and gets louder as you drive around a bend, the problem could be a dry universal joint. If this is the case, you'll have to have the joint replaced (once you hear the squeak, it's too late to lubricate it).

Squeal

Loose fan belts make a high-pitched squeal when you first start the engine; the squeal gets worse when you speed up or drive slowly around a turn, and your steering wheel jerks. You can try to fix this problem yourself by spraying on a can of belt dressing. However, if the squealing continues, don't keep adding more dressing—you'll gum up the works. Take the car to the repair shop.

Thump

If you hear a steady thumping sound that changes in frequency as you slow down or speed up and you don't have a stowaway in your trunk, your car probably has a problem with a tire, which could be developing a bubble. If you keep on going, you could have a flat tire.

Ticking

If every time your car idles it sounds as though you're being pursued by the crocodile from *Peter Pan*, suspect a cracked flywheel. The bigger the crack, the noisier the tick, which should stop whenever you start moving. If you hear this noise, drive to the repair shop immediately; if the flywheel breaks, you'll have to tow the car in.

Whizzing

A high-pitched whizzing or whining when you start the engine indicates that the starter drive or solenoid is defective. See your mechanic.

IF YOU SMELL A RAT

Sometimes malfunctioning cars stink. Certain distinctive smells indicate certain problems, so take a whiff. The quicker you can diagnose your own problem, the easier your life will be.

A COMPLETE WASTE OF TIME

The 3 Worst Things to Do when Your Car Starts Its Own Symphony of Noise:

1. Pretend you didn't hear anything.

2. Turn up the radio.

3. Assume it will take care of itself.

Gas

If you smell gasoline, you've got a leak somewhere in the fuel system. It could be something as simple as a flooded engine. Otherwise, if the gas is leaking from the fuel pump, fuel lines, or the gas tank, you'll see a puddle of gas lying under the car. If you can't see anything leaking underneath, check around under the hood. A gas leak in the carburetor or fuel-injection system may spill onto the top of the engine, where you might be able to see it. (Sometimes, the leak is underneath other parts and won't be visible.) Gas leaks can be dangerous, so you should take your car into the repair shop right away. If the leak isn't a flood and the repair shop isn't too far away, you can drive there instead of having your car towed.

Hot Oil

If you've ever pulled into your garage and smelled that "hot metal" smell, you could have some oil leaking on to the exhaust pipe. Leaks could be coming from the engine, transmission, or power steering, so have your mechanic check.

Burning Toast

If you're driving along and suddenly you smell burning English muffins, you could have a smoldering wire. You can drive your car to the repair shop to have the smell pinpointed unless the smell is strong—then have the car towed. If the smell is very strong, disconnect the battery to remove the source of electricity.

Sulfur (or Rotten Eggs)

This smell can be traced to a malfunctioning emissions control system (specifically, the catalytic converter). This malfunction occurs when the car isn't burning fuel correctly and can plug up your catalytic converter. Seek help on this one. Overcharging the battery causes a similar odor.

Sweetish Smell

That sickening sweet smell is probably due to leaking coolant (a mixture of water and antifreeze). You can open the hood and check this problem out yourself, but be careful if the engine is hot. Look for a leak anywhere at the radiator, the hoses, or the water pump. If you notice this smell with the blower fan on, you may have a leak in the heater core. You can replace a leaky hose yourself once the car has cooled down, or get your mechanic to do it, but don't ignore the problem: leaking coolant can make your car overheat.

Brake Smell

This nasty smell comes from overheating brakes or a slipping clutch, and it's something you can't miss. Try to figure out which wheel it's coming from and see whether the wheel is hot. If there's only a slight odor right after you've had new brakes put on, it should go away in a day or so. If you've been driving in heavy traffic and you've been riding the brakes, they may get hot enough to smell, but they'll stop once they cool down. If the smell continues, however, it could be a problem with sticking disc pads (disc brakes) or a sticking wheel cylinder (drum brakes). Either way, your brakes are dragging and over-heating. Drive to the repair shop or have the car towed.

Musty Odor

If you get in your car and smell damp, musty air, you've got moisture trickling in somewhere and dampening your carpet or upholstery. Check for leaks around the windows or inside the trunk. If the area stays damp, you're asking for mold and mildew to set in, so dry out the area (either leave the windows open on a sunny day or use an electric fan or hair dryer).

If you've got broken window seals that are leaking moisture, get some black silicon for sealing leaks and squirt it in there as you would caulk a bathtub. In the future, don't park in the hot sun, which causes the rubber on the seals to dry out and crack.

YOU'VE GOT LEAKAGE!

You know the feeling: You park your car, and when you move it the next day, there's a big ugly puddle on your garage floor. You've got leakage! Here's how to tell what's coming from where:

Antifreeze   This green, yellow, or bright orange fluid has a sweet odor (old coolant may be brown or black). If you see this stuff, check around the radiator, radiator hoses, engine core plugs, and the water pump.

Automatic transmission fluid   If you see this light red-to-brown oil, look for leaks around the pan and external seals.

QUICK ⬭ PAINLESS

If you've got a lingering musty odor after drying out the car, try a deodorant spray designed for a car's interior or a dryer softener sheet.

Battery acid   If you smell rotten eggs in the puddle, it's probably sulfuric acid leaking from the battery. This acid can burn, so if you get it on your skin or clothes, flush the area with water.

Brake fluid   If the puddle looks like water but it's not, it's brake fluid. If you see this puddle on your floor, get to a repair shop right away.

Diesel fuel   If the fluid smells like your home heating oil, but it's coming from your car, it's diesel oil. Check around the injector pump, fuel filter, and fuel lines for a leak.

Gas   Everybody knows this smell. Look for leaks under the hood, around the gas tank, and along fuel lines.

Gear oil   If the fluid is tan to dark black and oily, it could be gear oil found in manual transmission fluid, axles, and differentials.

Power steering fluid   If you have an old car, it uses automatic transmission fluid in the steering system; newer cars use a special power steering fluid that's thinner than fresh motor oil but has the same color.

Shock absorber fluid   A dark stain on the shock body gives this one away. If a shock is leaking, replace it. (Shocks are best replaced in pairs.)

Windshield wiper solvent   Bright blue and smelling like detergent or alcohol, this stuff can leak out of a cracked reservoir or a leaky hose. Remember that this solvent is poisonous.

IF YOU'RE SO INCLINED

Try to keep a stash of extra fluids accessible and you'll be far along the road to keeping your car happy and healthy!

Getting Time on Your Side

	The Old Way	The Lazy Way
Fixing a hiss	10 minutes	5 minutes
Fixing a musty smell	5 minutes	1 minute
Detecting a gas leak	10 minutes	5 minutes
Identifying a smell	Not until it's too late	2 minutes
Identifying a noise	Not until it's too late	2 minutes
Locating the problem	Where do I start?	10 minutes

nine

Don't Be Fueled: Fuel Systems

One of the most important parts of maintaining the car isn't what you do to the car, but what you put into it. Odds are, most of the money you're spending on your car is going into fuel, so it pays to understand how the fuel system works. And now that almost nobody uses full-service stations anymore, we're the ones putting the gas into the tank, no matter how lazy we're feeling.

ANATOMY OF A FUEL SYSTEM

Although you put liquid gas into the tank of the car, the gas must be transformed into a vapor before the car can start. The fuel system funnels the fuel to the combustion area and turns the liquid gas into vapor. The following sections describe the car parts responsible for this transformation.

Fuel Tank

The fuel tank is where the liquid gas is stored. You can tell how much gas is in there by looking at the gas gauge on the

A COMPLETE WASTE OF TIME

The 3 Worst Things to Do when It Comes to Your Car:

1. Assume you don't need to know how it works.

2. Actually believe there are little hamsters in the wheels that are running around to make your car go.

3. Don't take care of it.

dash, which is connected to a floating sending unit in the tank.

Fuel Pump

Your fuel pump's job is to move fuel from the tank to either the carburetor or the fuel injection system. On its way, fuel flows through a fuel filter to screen out contaminants. The engine draws in air, which is mixed with a fine spray of fuel from either a carburetor or a fuel-injection system, depending on your type of car.

Carburetor

The carburetor is one of two ways that a car can mix fuel and air prior to combustion. Older cars mix fuel in the carburetor, which draws in air from the outside and passes it through an air filter that snags dirt before the air moves down through the carburetor to mix with liquid gas. The result of this mixing is vapor that moves on to the combustion chamber.

Fuel-Injection System

Newer cars mix air and fuel in a fuel-injection system, which began to appear in most cars in the 1980s with the advent of sophisticated computers. A fuel-injection system mixes air and fuel in the combustion chamber or in a series of passages called the intake manifold, which is located just outside the combustion chamber. In a top-functioning car, the fuel/air mixture is just right, so you get the best possible gas mileage. Computers in some fuel-injection systems can be extremely complex, controlling the flow of fuel depending on speed, temperature, and air pressure inside and outside the intake manifold.

GETTING THE MOST OUT OF YOUR FUEL SYSTEM

You don't want to let the fuel level get too low in your car. Obviously, you've got more important things to do than walk to the gas station lugging a heavy gas can, but there's another reason. All gas contains contaminants (including some condensation and dust) that sink to the bottom of the gas tank as you drive. The lower your fuel level falls, the greater the chance that these contaminants will get sucked up into the fuel delivery system, which could damage the components. Keep your tank at least a quarter full, and you won't have to worry about what's floating around in your fuel lines. What you can worry about is the type of gas you select.

Octane Fuel: How Much Bang for Your Buck?

Contrary to what Madison Avenue tries to say, your car is probably going to run just great on regular old 87 octane gas. If you spring for a higher octane fuel, you're just throwing your dollars down the gas tank. Premium fuel isn't any better than regular fuel; it doesn't have more additives or detergents, and it won't make your car run stronger or better or longer. All octane does is to regulate the engine's combustion, which is how the engine burns fuel. Octane is the measure of the fuel's resistance to pinging, although other factors also affect octane capabilities.

YOU'LL THANK YOURSELF LATER

Keep a fully charged class B fire extinguisher handy whenever you work on your fuel system.

Different engines require different octane levels, so check your owner's manual for the octane rating that's right for your car. Don't buy a higher-octane gas than you need—you're wasting your money—and don't choose a lower octane than you need to save money— you'll get poor performance and higher operating costs. Follow Goldilocks' example, and choose the octane rating that's just right for your car. The only time you'd want to spring for premium gas in a typical car is if your engine starts knocking at highway speeds.

Fill 'Er Up!

Now that you know exactly what kind of fuel to use, it's time to think about how you fill the tank. You've probably filled your tank thousands of times, but there's always something new to learn. Here are a few tips to remember when you're fulfilling this very basic task:

- Don't breathe the fumes as you're refueling. They'll make you sick.

- Don't overfill the tank. You can round off the cost of the gas, but don't go overboard. Only 90 percent of the tank should be filled so that there's some empty space for the vapors to expand.

- If you dribble some gas onto the car, don't rub it off; if you do rub it, you risk staining the paint. Instead, flush the spot with water as soon as you can.

Diesel Fuel

The main difference between a diesel and a gas engine lies in the fuel system. If you've got a diesel car, your fuel

QUICK n° PAINLESS

Check your manual for what kind of gas you need and save yourself some money.

is thick and not very volatile. Your engine uses a mechanical diesel-injection pump to inject fuel into the cylinders that already are charged with highly compressed, heated air. The high temperature (not the spark plugs) triggers the diesel fuel to burn.

But What About Mileage?

Whether you drive your car only a few miles a day or you're a marathon commuter, fuel economy is important. It's especially important to those of us with more important things to do than pull over to pump gas every few miles. Fortunately, there are some things you can do to make sure your fuel system is working properly:

1. Get regular tune-ups. Tests show that almost anyone can improve fuel consumption by at least 10 percent just by doing regular maintenance and tune-ups. A major spark plug manufacturer found that 8 out of every 10 cars will have some maintenance deficiency that directly affects fuel economy, emissions, or performance. Most of this mileage-robbing neglect can be prevented with regular maintenance: check your oxygen sensors, air filter, spark plugs, and wires and get tune-ups as required.

2. Check tire pressure often—once a week at least.

3. Try to combine short trips; it's a more efficient use of your time, and you'll get better gas mileage. If you make a bunch of short trips of less than five miles (especially in cold weather), your engine never has a chance to warm up and work efficiently.

Congratulations! You've kept your car tuned up and improved its efficiency! Now relax and go take a nap!

The Lazy Way

4. Check your brakes. Brake rotors or drum brake calipers that rub, or brake shoes that don't release properly can eat into fuel economy.

5. Turn off the air conditioner. Any electrical gadgets drain fuel, but you can't do away with your headlights or defoggers. It's the air conditioning that really guzzles the gas.

6. Don't use wider tires than are recommended for your car. Wider tires use more gas because they cause more friction against the road.

7. Use overdrive or fifth gear whenever you can.

8. Avoid driving in wind, bad road conditions, heavy traffic, rough terrain, or with a lot of passengers.

MAINTAINING YOUR FUEL SYSTEM

Spending just a few moments now and then on your car's fuel system will pay big dividends in your car's economy and reliability. If you don't want trouble—and what lazy car owner does?—then it pays to read the following sections.

Replacing the Fuel Filter

As you read earlier in this chapter, the fuel filter's job is to keep gunk out of your carburetor or fuel-injection system. To make sure everything stays clean, once a year you must replace your paper or metal mesh fuel filter. Unfortunately, you won't be able to see inside the filter canister to know when the filter gets dirty. If your car sputters when you're driving at high speeds and then stops bucking when you slow down, your fuel filter probably needs changing. The fuel filter can eventually get so dirty that your car won't run at all, so don't neglect this problem. If you have a car with a fuel-injection system, it's a good idea to have the experts change the filter, because high pressure in the gas lines can spray gas in your face as you change the filter. Those of you with older carbureted cars can do the job yourself, however.

Changing the Fuel Filter in a Carbureted Car

You'll usually find the fuel filter in the top of the engine, somewhere between the fuel pump and the fuel-mixing system. If you see something that looks like a metal flour canister, that's the fuel filter. To change a fuel filter in a carbureted car, you'll need:

Owner's manual
Screwdriver or pliers
New fuel filter

1 Read your manual to find the location of your fuel filter.

2 Loosen the hose clamps on each side of the filter with your screwdriver or pliers, depending on the type of clamp used.

3 Remove the filter.

QUICK ⬭ PAINLESS

You can buy a replacement fuel filter at an auto parts store or hardware shop. There should be a brand name and parts number on the filter. Check your manual to make sure you've got the right one for your car.

Congratulations! You've replaced the fuel filter. Now take a break and go get a cone of rocky road ice cream. You deserve it!

The Lazy Way

4 Install the new filter, making sure the arrow points toward the fuel delivery system (the direction of flow to the engine).

5 When you replace the filter, check all the other fuel lines and hoses.

6 Start the engine and check for leaks.

Replacing the Air Filter

There's nothing easier to change than an air filter, so there's no excuse for driving around with a gunky one. If you don't change a dirty one in time, you'll get poor gas mileage, and if you really fall down on the job, the car won't start at all. A dirty air filter makes the air/fuel mixture too rich and can increase fuel consumption as much as 10 percent. Tests show that a third of all cars have dirty air filters.

How often you change the filter depends on where you're driving, but many folks do it once a year. A new air filter usually costs less than $10, so why not? Of course, you should check your owner's manual for a guideline, but use your head, too. If you live on a clear, clean mountaintop, your air filter will have less work to do than if you commute through Death Valley or drive through windy construction sites.

To check the filter, you must first find it. In carbureted cars, the air filter is sitting in a big round device above the carburetor. Fuel-injected cars keep the air filter in a large hose between the car's front grill and the engine.

1. For carbureted cars: Remove the wing nut on the lid of the air cleaner and lift off the top to expose the filter. For fuel-injected cars: Remove the clips or nuts on the filter cover and lift out the filter.

2. Check to see whether the filter is dirty.

3. Clean out the air cleaner housing with an old cloth (or vacuum it if it's really filthy).

4. Pop in a new filter. In a carbureted car, the filter can be inserted correctly with either side up. Filters for a fuel-injected car can only go in one way.

5. Eye the new filter to make sure it's level.

6. Replace and tighten the fasteners on the air cleaner or filter cover.

FUEL SYSTEM PROBLEMS

It may not have mattered so much back in the days when Henry Ford was driving his Model T, but today's modern engines require a well-functioning fuel system in order to work properly. A problem with the fuel system isn't always obvious at first. Symptoms that can be caused by the fuel system can also be related to other problems in other car systems entirely. However, if you suddenly notice you've only been getting about five miles to the gallon, it could be due to one or more of the following problems.

IF YOU'RE SO
INCLINED

Feeling really lazy? You can get a lifetime air filter for slightly more money. These drop-in air filters fit the same as the original filter. You simply clean them periodically and use them over and over.

Hesitation on Acceleration

This problem could be caused by a dirty carburetor or fuel filter, an improper accelerator pump setting, bad ignition timing, or fouled spark plugs.

Sluggish Performance

If your car just seems to have lost its zip, it could be due to fuel system problems such as a dirty fuel or air filter, bad ignition timing, or an automatic choke adjustment problem. The cause also could be worn spark plugs.

Stalls Often

You're sitting in traffic, and when you hit the gas pedal, the engine stops. This problem could be caused by a dirty air or fuel filter or an automatic choke adjustment problem.

Won't Start

If you stuck in your key and the engine turned over and then quit, it's not your battery or starter. If you smell gas, you could have flooded the engine. The solution to this problem is a lazy car owner's dream: jut sit there and wait for 10 to 15 minutes. The fuel will evaporate, and then you can start the car by doing these steps:

1. Press the gas pedal and hold it down; don't pump the pedal.

2. Turn the ignition key and crank the engine until it starts.

3. Release the gas pedal.

A COMPLETE WASTE OF TIME

The 3 Worst Things to Do when Your Car Starts Acting Strange:

1. Ignore it.

2. Say "I'll look at it tomorrow."

3. Don't pay attention to what those warning signs are really telling you.

Sputtering/Coughing

If your engine runs rough as it idles or when you step on the gas, it could be caused by dirt in the fuel lines or problems with emissions control equipment.

Getting Time on Your Side

	The Old Way	The Lazy Way
Filling the gas tank	10 minutes	5 minutes
Changing the fuel filter	30 minutes	20 minutes
Changing the air filter	2 hours	5 minutes
Time spent walking to the gas station since you ran out of gas	Hours	Never again
Amount of times you have to refuel each week	Too often	Half the time
Driving with an inefficient fuel system	Every day	Never again

The Twice-A-Year Braking System Checkup

More than a third of all the cars flying down the road have brake problems, according to the National Car Care Council. If you don't want yours to be one of them and you don't want have to spend a lot of time fussing around with drums and discs, have your brakes checked at least twice a year (check your owner's manual for details).

The brakes are something you can have checked at your repair shop, or you can peek at your own pads if you want to save time at the shop. Checking your brakes is the best way to keep your car safe without expending lots of energy.

HOW BRAKES WORK

Your car has brakes so you can slow down and stop without sticking your leg out the door and dragging your foot on the ground. When you step on the brake, you create friction

between brake linings and the disc or drum brake unit at each of your wheels. As you press on the brake pedal, you're causing a plunger in the master cylinder to pump, which creates pressure in the brake lines. At the end of the brake lines, the pressure forces out wheel cylinder pistons or caliper pistons, creating the force that moves disc brake pads or drum brake shoes into contact with blade rotors or drums.

There are two basic types of brakes: drum brakes and disc brakes. Disc brakes can stop faster and run cooler, and almost any car built in the last 10 years has a combination of disc brakes on the front and drum brakes on the rear.

Drum Brakes

Drum brakes are controlled by fluid under pressure. When you slam on the brakes, you're forcing fluid from the master cylinder to smaller cylinders in each of the wheels, which forces the brake shoes against the moving drum bolted to the wheels.

Disc Brakes

If you know how hand brakes work on a bike, then you also know how disc brakes operate on a car. When you step on your car's brake pedal, you're applying a lot of force to both sides of a spinning disc (also called a rotor) on which the wheels are mounted. Brake pads are held in place by calipers, which squeeze the pads against the disc when you step on the brake. The car slows and then stops.

Power Brakes

Stopping a big car can be difficult, so many modern vehicles come equipped with power brakes, making it easier for the motorist to stop the car. With power brakes, when you step on the brake pedal, you activate a power booster, which helps you apply the brakes. However, the engine has to be running for the power boosters to work. If the engine stops for some reason, you're going to lose all that extra power, and it will be much harder to stop the car.

ABS Brakes

There's a right way to handle emergencies. If you skid, you should turn into the skid to escape. If you're driving down the road and a deer leaps out in front of your car, you should not slam on the brakes. The reality, however, is that when emergencies happen people don't always do what they should. When you encounter a problem while driving and that adrenaline starts pumping, you are likely to go for the brakes and push the pedal to the floor. Chances are good that when you do that, you'll go right into a skid.

Realizing that it was futile to try changing a person's natural fear reactions, manufacturers invented ABS brakes to take advantage of the fact that people react with panic in these situations. With ABS (anti-lock brake system) brakes, you're supposed to slam on the brakes in an emergency; when you do, a computer that controls each wheel separately will step in and pump the brakes much faster than you could hope to do. This action helps stabilize the car.

IF YOU'RE SO INCLINED

Check your brakes every few months and you'll save yourself a lot of headaches later on!

ABS brakes sound like a good idea, but experts point out that these brakes haven't seemed to lessen the number of car crashes. Your brain is still the best computer out there, so even if you've got ABS brakes, you still need to use your head.

Parking Brake

This type of brake is mechanical and includes cables from the lever or pedal (depending on whether it's a hand or foot brake) to the rear wheels. If you've got disc brakes, the cables pull the pads tightly to the rotor. In drum brakes, the cables pull the brake shoes against the drum. No matter which type of brakes you have, be sure to engage this brake every time you park. If you don't use it often, the cables can rust, and then the brake will be pretty useless.

An Ounce of Prevention

Brakes can't last forever, but you can make them last much longer than they usually do. The secret is: don't ride your brakes! Nothing is harder on your brakes than heat and pressure; these factors will make them work harder and wear out much faster.

Also, avoid slamming your brakes. You can imagine that if you tried to stop your bike by grabbing the wheels with a gloved hand at top speed, you'd soon wear out your gloves. But slowly touching the wheel will still slow down the bike, without wearing out the gloves nearly as fast. The same thing happens when you pump the brakes when you want to slow down instead of stomping them

A COMPLETE WASTE OF TIME

The 3 Worst Things to Do with Your Parking Brake:

1. Forget to engage the brake when you stop.

2. Forget to disengage the brake when you start.

3. Set the brake after driving in slush and snow, so the ice builds up around the cable.

to the floor. The car stops, and you don't wear down the brakes as quickly.

BRAKE PROBLEMS

A malfunctioning radio or broken air conditioner can be annoying, but failing brakes put you in a life-threatening situation. When you start to get signals from the brakes that something's amiss, rush your car into the service shop ASAP.

The Squeaky Brake

If you hear an occasional squeal from your disc brakes, it's not a hamster turning around in there; it's normal brake noise. If brakes squeal all by themselves when they're not being used, it's time for routine brake service. Horrendous screeching or shuddering could indicate brake pad or shoe problems.

Rear Clicking

If you release the brake and then hear an ominous clicking from the rear of the car (or a squeak every time you step on the pedal), the problem could be a lack of grease on the rear brake shoe backing plate. Get it fixed; it can lead to overheated and locked brakes.

Dragging Brakes

If your brakes pull, grab, drag, lock, or otherwise try to take over the control of your car, you need to have them checked out right away. The problem could be hydraulic fluid leaking onto the brakes, collapsed brake hoses, a wheel cylinder malfunction, or a sticking caliper.

YOU'LL THANK YOURSELF LATER

Don't wait! When your brakes start complaining, head straight for your mechanic!

Flashing Brake Light

If you start the engine and the warning brake light is still on, you could have a problem with low brake fluid or faulty hydraulic pressure.

Mushy Brakes

When you step on the brake, and the pedal gets all squishy, it could mean that there's not much fluid left in your hydraulic brake system. This problem could be caused by some malfunction in the master or wheel cylinders, so head for the repair shop right away (if it's safe to do so).

Stubborn Pedal

The opposite of a mushy pedal is one that doesn't want to depress at all. This problem could be caused by a malfunction in the power brake system, a worn brake lining, or out-of-adjustment brakes. Again, drive directly to your repair shop if you can do so safely.

The Nightmare: You Can't Stop

Everybody's worst fear involves flying downhill into an intersection with a totally useless brake pedal. Fortunately, the chances that all four brakes will fail at once is slim. If you do have problems stopping, don't risk a drive to your mechanic unless the shop is next door; get towed to the shop.

If you find yourself in this dreadful situation, do the following:

■ Pump the brake pedal—fast.

Congratulations! You've learned how to handle your car in a braking emergency! Now treat yourself to a walk in the park!

The Lazy Way

- If you're not slowing down, downshift into second gear—and then into first.

- You may still be moving, but you will have slowed down. Now, *gently* apply the parking brake.

MAINTAINING YOUR BRAKES

As we've said earlier, most brake work should be done by professionals. However, if you want, you can check your brake fluid level and the linings. Remember that breathing asbestos dust from worn brake linings can cause lung cancer. Get a professional brake mechanic with the right equipment to remove asbestos brake dust.

Check that Brake Fluid

Your brakes depend on fluid to give that hydraulic push to help stop the car. Without brake fluid, the brakes can't stop the car, which is why it's important for even the busiest of drivers to occasionally take a peek at the brake fluid level. Be careful not to add transmission or power steering fluid to the brake fluid by mistake. These fluids can cause the brake fluid to boil and can ruin rubber components.

You need to check the level because as your brake linings wear, brake fluid flows into the wheel brake cylinders, and the fluid level in the reservoir drops slowly. If you don't add more brake fluid, eventually the level in the reservoir will drop too low.

When it's time to check the brake fluid level (every couple of months or at one of your oil changes), look for the master cylinder, bolted to the power brake booster

QUICK **π** *PAINLESS*

Review these tips on what to do if your brakes fail you now and you'll keep yourself and your family safe if you're ever in an emergency!

A COMPLETE WASTE OF TIME

The 3 Worst Things to Do when It Comes to Your Brakes:

1. Don't check them.

2. Slam on them all the time.

3. Ignore your brake fluid.

on the driver's side of the car. That's where the reservoir for the brake fluid is. Then follow these steps:

1. Wipe the lid of the reservoir so that no dirt falls into the fluid when you remove the cover.

2. Unfasten the fastening wire on the reservoir (you may need a pair of pliers or a screwdriver). Newer cars have a screw-on or push-on cap over a plastic reservoir.

3. Check the fluid level. It shouldn't be any lower than half an inch below the top of the reservoir. (There may be a "recommended level" marked on the outside of the plastic reservoir.)

4. If the level is low, add only the type of brake fluid your manual recommends. Pour it from a fresh sealed container.

If your brake fluid is low, you can assume that your brake linings are probably worn or there's a leak somewhere in the brake system, because brake fluid doesn't just evaporate into thin air. If your brake linings are worn, you'll need to get them fixed soon, or you'll risk damaging your rotors or brake drums. If the brake fluid is leaking somewhere and you don't fix it, you'll notice that your car gets harder and harder to stop. Eventually, you won't be able to stop it at all.

My Pad or Yours?

If you've got disc brakes, it's important to replace the pads when they get worn before they damage your rotor. If you're really lazy, you'll buy a car with built-in sensors that warn you when the pads are worn. Otherwise, you need to visibly check the pads every 10,000 miles. If you're very hard on your car and regularly drive up and down big mountains (or you do lots of stop-and-go driving), check your pads more often.

Checking Brake Pads

When you're working on your brakes, work on only one wheel at a time. Otherwise, the pistons could come out of the other caliper. You'll need:

Wheel chocks

Screwdriver

Jack handle or socket wrench

Jack and jack stand

Brake cleaner

New brake pads

C-clamp

1 Put on the parking brake and brace the car with chocks under the wheels.

2 Remove the wheel covers from the front wheels with a screwdriver.

3 Using the wrench end of the jack handle or a socket wrench, loosen the lug nuts on both front wheels one turn.

4 Jack up the front of the car until the wheels are off the ground and put the jack stands under the car.

5 Remove the lug nuts, the wheel, and the tire assembly.

Congratulations! You've checked your brake fluid. Now go take a drive in the country and relax!

The Lazy Way

6. Inspect both sides of the rotor for wear, cracks, and rust. If you find any of these, consult a mechanic.

7. Locate the inspection hole on the caliper, which lets you see both linings and detect wear without removing the caliper. (If your pads' friction material is riveted, you can't judge the extent of wear using the inspection hole. You'll have to remove the pads to do this; follow the service manual for your car.)

8. Pads should be no thinner than $1/16$ of an inch; if they are, remove them.

9. Clean the caliper, disc, and brake assembly with brake cleaner.

10. Inspect the dust boot for cracks or cuts and check for signs of moisture. Be sure all parts are dry before replacing the pads.

11. To replace the pads, first push the piston back in the caliper with a C-clamp.

12. Remove the pads from both sides of the disc and install new pads.

13. Be careful not to force fluid out of the reservoir onto your paint. If you've topped off the fluid, there may be more in the system than you need. Place a clean rag over the top of the reservoir when retracting pistons.

14. When you're finished, pump the brake pedal until the pads touch the rotor. They will self-adjust. Then recheck the fluid level.

Bleeding the Brakes

Once you've refilled the brake fluid and replaced the brake pads, you should bleed the brakes. You should do

this any time a line has been opened, because air in the hydraulic system can reduce braking efficiency. Brakes should be bled at least once every two years to remove built-up moisture and contaminants that can rust and gum up brake hydraulic parts. However, if you're unsure at all about brake work, don't do it yourself.

Follow your service manual, but usually this is how you bleed brakes:

1. Have a friend press on the brake pedal while you open the bleed fitting on each wheel cylinder or caliper.

2. Connect a hose from the bleed fitting into a container of clean brake fluid.

3. Close the bleed fitting once clean brake fluid flows instead of air bubbles.

4. Repeat the process at each wheel to remove air from the brake lines; follow the bleeding sequence specified for your car.

IF YOU'RE SO
INCLINED

When you replace the pads, you may also want to replace the pins, springs, and clips. You can buy a brake pad kit that contains pads and all this hardware.

Getting Time on Your Side

	The Old Way	The Lazy Way
Checking brake fluid	20 minutes	10 minutes
Checking brake pads	1 hour	20 minutes
Keeping your brakes in tip-top shape	Uh oh!	30 minutes
Troubleshooting your brakes	Uh oh!	20 minutes
Extending your brake life	Who knew?	Every day

Chapter eleven

Current Events: Electrical Systems

Your car may run on gas, but without electricity you'd just be sitting in a pile of metal on wheels, heading nowhere. The electrical system includes not just the obvious—lights and other accessories—but also the battery, starter, and the ignition system.

Although every car's engine is fueled by gas, it's powered by electricity. The source of that power is the battery and alternator. When the engine starts to run, an electric spark ignites the air/fuel mixture, and you're off! When it comes to the electrical system, there will be some items you can handle yourself, and some things you need to leave to the professionals.

THE CHARGING CIRCUIT

Your battery is the source of power in your car, and it's got two jobs to do. It stores electricity so you can start and run

your car, and it also operates all those fun accessories when your engine isn't running. Anyone who has ever bopped to the Blues Brothers when the engine was off but the key was turned to "on" knows what that is all about.

A battery's energy isn't infinite, however, and eventually when the power is used up, the battery will be ineffective. That's why your car has an alternator. When you step on the gas and start the car, the alternator produces electricity and recharges the battery (the one you've been running down listening to the radio while the engine is off). The alternator's boss is the voltage regulator, which tells the alternator when to produce energy and how much to give.

If you've ever jumped a battery, you know that there are positive and negative terminals on the top (or side) of the battery. The positive terminal connects to the starting circuit, and the negative terminal is connected via cable to a ground (usually the engine block). You need the ground to complete the circuit and allow the current to flow.

Yearly Battery Maintenance

You car owners without a lot of time on your hands will be happy to know that today's cars usually have either low- or no-maintenance batteries. This means you don't need to spend a lot of time fooling around with the electrolyte levels in the battery, checking the levels, and so on. In fact, these no-maintenance batteries are sealed up tighter than an oyster with a pearl, and you couldn't add water if you wanted to. There's no such thing as a free lunch, however; even a maintenance-free battery needs some attention once a year.

Checking Your Battery

Once a year, you need to clean off the battery terminals. Here's what you need to have on hand to do the job:

Wrench

Battery terminal puller

Wire battery brush, steel wool, or wire brush

Baking soda

Water

Rag

Hydrometer (that thing that looks like a turkey baster)

White grease or petroleum jelly

1 Loosen the nuts on the battery terminals at the end of the cable.

2 Remove the negative terminal with your battery cable terminal puller.

3 Scrub off corrosion on the battery post and cable clamp or terminal with a wire brush or steel wool.

4 Remove the positive terminal and clean the battery post and cable connector.

5 Clean the battery cover with a rag dipped in a mixture of baking soda and water.

6 Check the condition of the battery cells using the hydrometer. Hold the hydrometer vertically, so the float bobs freely and doesn't touch the inner walls of the

YOU'LL THANK YOURSELF LATER

A dirty battery case will lessen the charge, because the dirt creates a path for the current to leak between the terminals. This slowly discharges the battery.

IF YOU'RE SO *INCLINED*

To avoid losing stored diagnostic codes and other data (clock, radio stations, engine functions, and so on) when you disconnect the battery, plug an inexpensive "memory unit" into your cigarette lighter to temporarily power these devices. (You can find one at any auto parts store.) Some radios with anti-theft features will lock up if power is interrupted and may need to be recoded.

hydrometer barrel. Consult the directions that come with the hydrometer to figure out the state of your battery's charge.

7 If the readings indicate a low charge, you might be able to have your battery recharged; if it's too low, you'll have to get a new battery.

8 Check the water level and add water if necessary.

9 Replace the cell cover.

10 Flush the case with a gentle stream of cool water; wipe dry.

11 Replace the positive terminal to its post first, and then replace the negative terminal. Tighten the bolts.

12 Apply a thin film of petroleum jelly to each post or terminal.

Replacing the Battery

Unfortunately, in some cases you just need to accept the fact that your battery's days are numbered, and it's time to buy a new one.

Putting in a New Battery

You can replace the battery on your own. Here's what you need:

Water

Wrench

Battery cable puller (if your battery has top posts)

Baking soda

Rag

New battery

1 Obtain the right size and capacity battery for your car.

2 Disconnect the battery terminals, negative terminal first.

3 Loosen the bolt on the clamp that holds the battery in place (look on the top or bottom of the battery).

4 Hoist the battery out of the car.

5 Clean the tray on which the battery sits with a rag dipped in a solution of water and baking soda and then dry.

6 Set the new battery onto the tray and tighten the clamp.

7 Clean the battery cables and reattach them, connecting the positive terminal first.

IGNITION SYSTEM

In order for the fuel/air mixture in your car's cylinders to be ignited, an electric spark must be delivered to the cylinders. The spark plugs are the devices that do this, supplying the fire that ignites the controlled explosions in your cylinders.

Changing Spark Plugs

You'll be happy to know that today's cars are so efficient you only need to worry your head about changing the

QUICK ⊞ PAINLESS

You can use platinum- or silver-tipped plugs instead of standard ones. They won't make your car run any better, but they will last longer. Platinum plugs can last up to 100,000 miles.

Mark your calendar for the next time you'll need to change your spark plugs so you won't forget!

plugs every couple of years (or every 25,000 miles, whichever comes first). Follow the recommended interval in your owner's manual if it differs from this recommendation.

Get Ready, Get Set, Change!

When you buy new plugs, consult your owner's manual and buy the type the manufacturer recommends. You'll need a complete set: four for a four-cylinder engine, six for a six-cylinder, and so forth. To put the new plugs in, you'll need this stuff:

Gap gauge

Spark plug connector puller (not always necessary)

Old paint brush

Spark plug wrench

New plugs

Torque wrench

1 Before you start, make sure your engine has been stopped for at least an hour, so it's cool.

2 Set the gap for all the spark plugs using your gap gauge. The gap between the center electrode and ground electrode on the side must be exactly the way the car maker recommends.

3 If the gap isn't right, you can gently bend the ground side electrode until it is.

4 Locate your old plugs. In today's cars, you may need to consult your owner's manual in order to find the spark plugs.

5 Remove the spark plug wire by gently pulling it. (If it doesn't come off easily, grab a spark plug connector puller to help.)

6 Sweep debris from around the plugs with the paint brush.

7 Remove the plugs with a spark plug wrench.

8 Install the new plug. Tip: Start plugs by hand to avoid cross-threading. Put a drop of oil or antiseize compound on the plugs' threads so you can remove the spark plugs easily the next time.

9 Tighten the plugs with a torque wrench or spark plug wrench. (Don't overtighten!)

10 Reattach the spark plug wires.

Replacing Spark Plug Wires

You'll be happy to hear that replacing spark plug wires is not something you have to do very often. You may not need to attempt this until your car is about five years old—it's the miles that count, and when your car has logged 50,000 miles, it's time to remove the old spark plug wires and put on some new ones.

You'll know that old spark plug wire bell is tolling when the engine starts to:

- Run harder
- Run rough
- Misfire (especially when loaded or wet)

YOU'LL THANK YOURSELF LATER

If you always forget to turn off your lights, you can buy an inexpensive warning buzzer that plugs into your fuse panel. It will warn you when you forget to flip the off switch.

- Guzzle gas

- Spit out more pollutants

Want other clues? If you look at the wires and they look cracked, oily, cut, frayed, charred, or otherwise bruised and abused, then it's time to replace them.

You'll need to buy a set of replacement wires at the local auto supply store. When you go shopping, remember that your mother was right: you get what you pay for. Don't buy cheap spark plug wires—if anything, buy something better than what came on your car in the first place. If you have a fairly new car, you can probably find replacement wire sets with molded wires, boots, and snap-on terminals, which is ideal for those of us without lots of time to waste. What you don't want to mess with are sets that will require you to cut everything to size yourself. Who's got the time for that?

Now, to Replace the Wire

Now that you've got your wire set, grab a cup of coffee and listen up. Here's what you need to do the job:

Masking tape or chalk

Spark plug wire puller

Spark plug wire set

New distributor cap

1 Label each wire and its terminal on the old distributor cap with bits of masking tape. This labeling saves you time trying to figure out which wire goes where.

Congratulations! You've changed your plugs and are ready to start on the wires! But take a break first and enjoy a nice cup of herbal tea.

The Lazy Way

2 You can pull and twist (gently!) each rubber part that goes over the spark plug (it's called a *boot*) to remove the wire, or you can use a spark plug wire puller.

3 Replace one wire at a time. Connect it to the plug and the new distributor cap.

4 Route the wires exactly the same way that the old ones went.

BROKEN TAILLIGHT

We've all done it: you're minding your own business and backing up, and suddenly you accidentally tap another car, a light pole, or a mailbox—and crack your taillight. If just a small piece of the taillight is missing, don't worry—there is a solution!

The Lazy Way to fix this problem is to go to your auto parts supply store, and buy lens repair tape. Cover the opening with the tape (you'll pay less than $2 at most places). Keep in mind that some states won't go along with this repair when it comes to inspection time. In this case, buy a good used lens for less than a new one.

FUSES: THE FINAL WORD

If you're having trouble with your electrical system, it could be a blown fuse. Fuses are meant to prevent current from damaging electrical components and wires. *The Lazy Way* to deal with a blown fuse is to always have a set of fuses on hand; the few extras that come packed in your car's fuse box may not be enough to tide you over.

A COMPLETE WASTE OF TIME

The 3 Worst Things to Do with a Spark Plug Wire:

1. Replace the wires without labeling them first.

2. Pull on the wire itself instead of the boot.

3. Take off all the old wires at the same time and then route them any way they fit.

IF YOU'RE SO
INCLINED

Mount a rear window brake light in your older car for safety. Buy a kit at your auto parts store. Wiring is easy; just follow the instructions in the kit.

Lots of times, a minor problem (such as a light, windshield wipers, horns, or radio not working) is the result of a blown fuse, and all you have to do is replace the fuse to solve the problem. (If the fuses keep on blowing, then you've got a short somewhere in your circuit that needs to be tracked down. Visit your repair shop for this one.) Use the correct capacity fuse when replacing fuses, not a higher one.

Fuses come in four types. Be sure you get the right kind for your car:

- Flat miniplug: fits well in crowded fuse panels of newer cars
- Flat regular plug
- Glass cylinder
- Glass cylinder with pointed ends (European cars)

After you've pulled the old fuse, you can hold it up to the light to see whether the element has melted. Alternatively, some fuse pullers allow you to test the fuse.

Getting Time on Your Side

	The Old Way	The Lazy Way
Changing the spark plugs	Every 25,000 miles	Every 100,000 miles
Maintaining the battery	Monthly	Yearly
Fixing a taillight	15 minutes	5 minutes
Replacing a fuse	15 minutes	2 seconds
Troubleshooting an electrical problem	Hours	30 minutes
Rewiring your spark plugs	an afternoon	20 minutes

Chapter twelve

Put the Power Back in Your Train

When you're talking power train, you mean the engine, transmission, driveshaft, and rear axle assembly. This long train of components carries power from the front to the back of your car.

HOW IT ALL WORKS

If you're driving an older car with rear-wheel drive, your transmission is directly behind the engine in the front of the car. It will have a long driveshaft with universal joints (U joints) at each end to make it flexible. The driveshaft connects the transmission to the rear end and the rear wheels.

A front-wheel drive car has a transaxle (where the transmission and differential are installed in a single housing). The engine may be mounted in front of the transaxle or alongside it. Two axles transfer power to the front wheels. Each axle has a CV joint on both ends to make it flexible.

In a four-wheel drive car, power can be supplied to all four wheels to increase traction in adverse conditions. In these cars, front-wheel drive and rear-wheel drive are combined in a single vehicle to drive all wheels.

Engine

The engine is the heart and soul of your car, the part that provides the power. The amount of power your engine puts out depends on how many cylinders the engine has, the type of fuel system it uses, and how much the gas vapor is compressed. Maybe you've even heard your mechanic talk about torque, which is the twist force produced by the car's turning crankshaft (the primary rotating part of an engine). The engine sends hot water to the heater and also creates the vacuum that operates power brakes and other accessories. The crankshaft drives the air conditioner, a water pump to cool the engine, a power steering pump, and an alternator to generate electricity.

Transmission

The transmission's job is to decide how much power your car needs, and then shift gears to provide that power. Cars are equipped either with a manual (standard) transmission or an automatic transmission. If your car has a manual transmission, you decide when to change gears, and you physically disengage the clutch to move from one gear to another. An automatic transmission chooses the gears on its own.

IF YOU'RE SO INCLINED

Spend a little time getting familiar with the parts of your car now, and the next time you have to work on it your project will go much faster!

Driveshaft

The transmission is connected to the cars' rear end via the driveshaft, which has universal joints at each end to absorb stress and motion.

Rear End

When the torque in your car gets to the rear end (or the differential), it goes through a series of gears that takes the power to the wheels. If you have a front-wheel drive car, the power goes to the front of the car; in a rear-wheel drive car, the power goes to the rear. If you're driving a four-wheel drive car, the power goes to all four wheels, which is why four-wheel drive cars can drive through just about any kind of terrain.

TRANSMISSION PROBLEMS

It's not fun when your transmission goes south, and having repairs done can be a costly experience. By doing some preventive maintenance up front, you can save yourself lots of headache and heartache down the road.

Remember, there are more than 3,000 parts in an automatic transmission, and the parts for some newer cars can cost 10 times as much as those for older cars. Just getting to the parts you need to look at to diagnose a problem can be extremely difficult. Because transmissions are such complex units, preventive maintenance is the key to keeping repair costs down.

Won't Budge

If your car won't move and the parking brake isn't on, your transmission fluid might be too low. This problem is

Congratulations! You've gotten to know your car! Now treat yourself to some ice cream!

The Lazy Way

fairly easy to fix: just add transmission fluid. After you do that, push or tow your car to the repair shop to find out why the transmission was losing fluid in the first place.

No High Gear

If your car balks when you try to shift it into high gear or if you're standing on the gas pedal and heading nowhere fast, suspect something minor such as a bad vacuum hose, cable, or electrical switch. Your mechanic can pinpoint this problem for you.

Slipping

If your engine takes off when you step on the gas but the car itself is just sitting there, it could be a slipping clutch (manual) or a low fluid level (automatic), or it could be an internal problem affecting the gear. Check for some free play at the clutch pedal on manual shift cars. There should be about a half-inch of free play. Push down on the pedal with your hand; it should move slightly before you feel resistance. The lack of free play can cause clutch slippage. *The Lazy Way* solution? Take the car to a mechanic.

Stuck on Park

You're huffing, you're puffing, but that darned automatic won't shift out of park. The trick is to apply the parking brake before you put the car into park. Here's *The Lazy Way* to prevent this problem:

1. With the engine running, stop the car and keep your foot on the brake.

2. Engage the parking brake.

3. Put the transmission into park.

4. Turn off the car.

   When you're ready to drive again, reverse the order:

1. Start the car with your foot on the brake.

2. Move the transmission out of park.

3. Release the parking brake.

CHANGING THE TRANSMISSION FLUID

Transmission fluid lubricates the transmission. In a car with automatic transmission, the fluid helps to transfer energy from the engine and keep the transmission cool. If you're looking for *The Lazy Way* to maintain your car, you won't want to mess with changing the transmission filter—head for the repair shop for that one. On the other hand, you're more than capable of checking your automatic transmission fluid, so you will know when it needs to be changed. Most experts recommend that you check it every 24,000 miles, but you should take a peep a little more often to make sure it doesn't need to be changed.

Checking the Transmission Fluid

Most people can find their oil dipstick in the dark, but the dipstick for the transmission fluid is another matter entirely. If you've got a rear-wheel drive car, look for the dipstick at the rear on the left side of the engine (as you

QUICK ⬛ PAINLESS

To head off major problems, the Automatic Transmission Rebuilders Association recommends that you have your transmission serviced every 12,000 miles.

face the car). In most cases, front-wheel drive cars have the dipstick on the right side of the engine (as you face the car). Now that you've found the dipstick, here's what to do:

1. Pull the dipstick out and drip a few drops of the transmission fluid onto a piece of white paper or paper towel.

2. Look at the color of the drops to determine whether your fluid needs to be changed or your transmission has some problems that need to be fixed (see the following list).

Fresh transmission fluid is bright red, and as it oxidizes, it changes color. The color of the fluid tells you about the state of your transmission fluid:

- Cherry red to pink: Normal.

- Milky: This color indicates that you have a leak in the transmission cooler inside the radiator, because your coolant is mixing with the transmission fluid. Run right down to your repair shop and get this problem fixed.

- Yellowish to tan: Time for a fluid change.

- Dark red-brown: Fluid that smells burnt needs to be changed.

- Particles: If you can see what looks like metal parts, this is not a good sign. Some metal debris is normal, but metal bits in your fluid can indicate lots of wear and possible transmission damage. Get a second opinion from your mechanic.

Measuring Transmission Fluid

Now that you've correctly identified the color of your transmission fluid, you need to find out how much of the stuff is left.

1. Warm up your car and park it on a level surface with the transmission lever in neutral or park, depending on the type of car you have. (Consult your owner's manual for this information.)

2. Have your engine idling as you check the transmission fluid.

3. Remove the transmission dipstick and wipe it on a paper towel. Push it all the way back down the tube.

4. Withdraw the dipstick again and read the level on both sides of the dipstick to make sure you're getting an accurate reading.

Adding Transmission Fluid

If your dipstick tells you that you've got to add more fluid, go ahead and top it off. Don't overfill the transmission fluid. If you put in too much, you'll create air bubbles. After you add fluid, check for leaks, because there must be some reason why you're losing fluid.

Topping It Off

If you need to add more transmission fluid, find out the type you need to add by reading the fine print on your dipstick or

YOU'LL THANK YOURSELF LATER

Change your fluid when it's reached the jaundice (yellow) stage. If you wait until it's black, you risk transmission failure.

IF YOU'RE SO
INCLINED

Test the transmission fluid level several times. Owners often misread the transmission fluid level. When in doubt, believe the lower reading.

consulting your owner's manual. To add more transmission fluid, you'll need:

Small-mouthed funnel

Fresh transmission fluid

1 With the funnel, pour fluid into the same tube where you insert the dipstick.

2 If a little is good, more is not always better: add fluid judiciously. Often, your dipstick will tell you how much you need to add. If it doesn't, add just a bit and then recheck your dipstick.

ENGINE PROBLEMS

If you're driving down the road and the car suddenly stalls, should you panic and run to the mechanic? It depends. Lazy car owners will be pleased to hear that if the car stalls only when it's really cold or only occasionally, you don't need to worry about it. Frequent stalling is more worrisome and could point to a problem in one of the following areas:

- Fuel system
- Electrical system
- Transmission

Your car is most likely stalling for one of the first two reasons, although a transmission problem could be the culprit, especially in newer cars. Suspect the transmission if the car stalls when it's been running, and then cools down and runs fine, but then stalls again after you've been running it.

Getting Time on Your Side

	The Old Way	The Lazy Way
Avoiding "park" problems	15 minutes	1 minute
Changing transmission fluid	2 hours	30 minutes
Finding the transmission fluid dipstick	Um, I swear I just saw it	2 seconds
Adding transmission fluid	1 hour	2 minutes
Stalling the engine	All the time	Once in a while
Troubleshooting high gear problems	Uh oh!	2 minutes

Chapter
thirteen

Effortlessly Exhausting the Possibilities

The exhaust system is the part of your car that handles the smelly, dirty burned gas vapor that's left over after your engine finishes burning fuel. There are a few things about your exhaust system that you can take care of yourself, which won't take too much time and can prevent lots of future hassles. Maintaining your exhaust system also can save your life. If carbon monoxide starts leaking into your car, it can make you sleepy or sick. Eventually, it can kill you.

WHAT THE EXHAUST SYSTEM DOES

The exhaust system routes the exhaust gases from the engine and muffles exhaust noise while keeping the gases from penetrating the passenger compartment. The exhaust system includes the exhaust manifold, exhaust pipes, catalytic converter, resonator, and muffler. No matter how plain or fancy the car you drive, your exhaust system functions in the same way: Burned gases flow from the engine through the exhaust ports into the exhaust manifold, where they're then funneled through the exhaust pipe, catalytic converter, and muffler. If you've got a resonator, the burned gases move through this device next and then on out of the car via the tailpipe.

Cars have either a single-exhaust system or a dual-exhaust system. Single-exhaust systems are the most common; dual-exhaust systems are noisier and are used mostly on V-type engines. In a dual-exhaust system, the two exhaust systems are separate, and they each contain a catalytic converter and muffler.

Exhaust Manifold

The exhaust manifold is made of cast iron or stainless steel and has lots of smooth, gentle bends to improve the flow of gases from the exhaust ports to the rest of the system. The exhaust manifold is bolted to the cylinder head and may have a heat control valve and an oxygen sensor.

Exhaust Pipes

The exhaust pipes connect the exhaust manifold, muffler, converter, and resonator that helps muffle exhaust noise. Most exhaust pipes are made of stainless steel, although some are flexible to allow for expansion and contraction.

Catalytic Converter

If you've got a car, you've also got a catalytic converter, which is usually bolted or clamped to the exhaust system. Cars may have one of two types of catalytic converters: One looks like a covered flat bowl, and the other looks

QUICK n' PAINLESS

Except for the tailpipe, any pipe you find under your car can be called an exhaust pipe.

like a tube-shaped honeycomb. After the exhaust gases leave the catalytic converter, they flow into the muffler, where the noise gets shushed up before passing into the tailpipe and out the rear of the car.

Muffler

The job of the muffler is to—surprise, surprise—muffle your exhaust noises. The muffler's job is to keep the engine noise down without causing too much back pressure.

Resonator

On some cars (especially larger luxury ones), the exhaust goes through another, smaller muffler called a resonator, located between the muffler and the tailpipe. The resonator is designed to quiet sound even more. Although resonators are usually attached near the end of the exhaust system, they can be found in front of the mufflers in some newer cars.

Tailpipe

At the tail end of the car is the tailpipe, which is probably welded to your muffler if you have a newer car. Some tailpipes contain resonators.

CHECKING THE EXHAUST SYSTEM

Exhaust systems last a lot longer these days because undercarriages are treated to prevent rust, but your exhaust system won't last forever. If your engine doesn't run well, for example, it can cause your converter to break down on the inside. It also doesn't help if you've

IF YOU'RE SO
INCLINED

Take a look at your exhaust system every now and then and you'll be able to keep it in top shape!

been playing Indiana Jones in your 4 x 4, bouncing over ruts and bumps. This kind of driving is very hard on a car's undercarriage, including the exhaust system. Short-hop driving, where the engine doesn't get up to the best operating temperature, allows condensation to form in the exhaust system. This condensation can lead to rust from the inside out.

Every once in a while, it's a good idea to check out the health of your exhaust system, so your exhaust system doesn't decide to check out on you. It doesn't take much time to scoot under your car's undercarriage and take a gander at what's going on under there, and it beats listening to the shriek of your muffler bouncing along the interstate!

Do this check twice a year:

1. Open the hood and check the exhaust manifold (there are two to check in a V6 or V8 engine).

2. Look for loose/missing mounting bolts or nuts, and check the mounting flange for cracks.

3. Make sure that the gaskets between the manifold and engine aren't broken or missing.

4. Look for holes, cracks, or deep dents in the connections to components of the emissions control system.

5. Check that the oxygen sensor is securely attached to the manifold and is not leaking.

6. Close the hood and move on to the undercarriage.

When you go crawling around underneath your car, pop on a pair of safety goggles or glasses to protect your eyes from falling bits of rust or metal.

7. Jack up the car safely and use jack stands.

8. With a big flashlight, examine the exhaust system for rust, wear, or loose parts. Follow the exhaust pipe from the manifold on back to the tailpipe. Shake or rap on converter and muffler to check for loose baffles or damaged converter catalyst.

9. Look for a buildup of mud, salt, and other debris.

10. Poke a screwdriver at each pipe and connection. If the screwdriver penetrates through surface rust, you should replace that part.

11. Check all rubber hangers for cracks, missing chunks, or breaks.

12. Check the ground under the car for puddles or evidence of leaks.

13. While you're under there, if you've got a front-wheel drive car, check for tears or breaks in the axle boots.

14. If you find something amiss, take the car to the repair shop for further checks.

TROUBLESHOOTING YOUR EXHAUST SYSTEM

There are a number of other ways to figure out if something is going on with your exhaust that shouldn't be. Any one of the following symptoms could indicate a problem with your exhaust system.

A COMPLETE WASTE OF TIME

The 3 Worst Things to Do when Checking Your Exhaust System:

1. Start your exhaust checkup when the engine and exhaust are hot.

2. Run the engine in a closed garage.

3. Don't bother to use jack stands; balance the car on a couple of boxes you've got lying around.

Noise

If your car is making an unusual noise, you could have a bad muffler that needs to be replaced. If the noise is a hissing sound, you may just have a hole in your exhaust pipe or a loose connection. (Or maybe you have a snake coiled up in there!) Take a look at the pipes, catalytic converter, muffler, or other parts for problems or broken hangers.

Rattles can be caused by loose baffles in the muffler or an element in the converter that is breaking up. To be sure about what's really going on, tap on the suspected component with a rubber mallet to confirm a rattle.

Overheating Engine

A damaged muffler or tailpipe can put pressure on the engine, which can lead to overheating or a loss of power.

What's That Smell?

If you get a whiff of burning oil in the vicinity of the engine, it might be that your crankcase breathing system is clogged and needs to be cleaned or replaced.

SMOKE GETS IN YOUR EYES

There are other ways to assess the health of the exhaust system without crawling under the car, of course. You can tell a lot about your exhaust system's health by spending a minute looking at what's coming out of the tailpipe.

Blue Smoke

If you see blue-gray smoke billowing out, your car is telling you that the engine is burning oil with the fuel. You may have gunked-up oil passages or malfunctioning valve stem seals. If you're looking at blue smoke, pay a visit to your mechanic. Filthy oil passages or problematic valve stem seals aren't something the lazy car owner—or any other untrained car owner—should mess with.

On the other hand, if all you're getting is just a bit of wispy blue smoke when you first start up the car, you don't need to panic or visit your repair shop. You might want to think about changing your oil more often, however.

Black Smoke

In addition to looking like something from the *Rocky Horror Picture Show,* dense black smoke rolling out of your tailpipe can mean one of several things:

- The air filter may be dirty. If it is, replace it with a new one (consult Chapter 9 to find out how).
- A choke butterfly in the carburetor may be malfunctioning or maladjusted. See your mechanic.
- The fuel-injection system could be malfunctioning. Again, see your mechanic.
- The car is burning too much gas in proportion to air. Need we say this once more? See your mechanic.

White Smoke

If you see puffy clouds of white smoke coming from the exhaust, either you have moisture in your exhaust system

YOU'LL THANK YOURSELF LATER

If anything is billowing out of your exhaust system, run, don't walk, to get it fixed now!

or you're burning transmission fluid in the engine. Either way, you need to take the car in for repairs.

Moisture can get in through a cracked engine head or engine block or a blown head gasket, and if you don't get it fixed, it can lead to engine performance problems. If the car is burning transmission oil, you'll probably need to take the car in for a new vacuum modulator.

MUFFLER RX

Now that we've discussed preventive maintenance, it's time to face up to what happens when you don't do this stuff ahead of time. What happens, of course, is that you could be driving along the road to the accompaniment of the horrible grinding, thumping, roaring noise of a dragging muffler/exhaust.

Tying Up Your Exhaust Pipe

This quick fix will tide you over until you get to the repair shop. You'll need:

    wire coat hanger or cord
    gloves
    towel

1 Bend a clothes hanger open.

2 Wearing gloves and protecting your hands with a thick towel or rag, wrap a cord or wire hanger around the offending part.

IF YOU'RE SO
INCLINED

You can buy pre-bent exhaust pipes to fit most modern cars, or you can pay a muffler shop to bend a pipe for you.

3 Feed the wire through a nearby bracket and tie it. Don't wrap anything around the driveshaft.

4 Get to your repair shop immediately.

Fixing a Hole in an Exhaust Pipe

If it seems like there's a handy repair kit for just about every car problem, you're right. These repair kits are the fast and easy way to fix lots of commonplace car problems, which is why we keep mentioning them in this book. You'll be happy to know that there is a muffler repair kit to fix those holes you occasionally get in an exhaust pipe. Most of these kits include tape or adhesive that you can use to temporarily plug up an exhaust pipe hole.

Replacing an Exhausted Exhaust

If your exhaust pipe is riddled with more holes than a chunk of Gorgonzola, go ahead and replace it—don't worry about trying to plug the holes. Here's how:

1. To remove the whole pipe, remove the bolts holding the pipe to the exhaust manifold. If you aren't replacing the entire pipe, loosen and remove clamps on the section you are replacing.

2. Loosen and remove hangers that hold the exhaust pipe to the car.

3. Replace the exhaust pipe and reconnect it to the system.

Congratulations! You've tied up your exhaust pipe. You must be exhausted! After you visit the repair shop, drive to your favorite restaurant and reward yourself.

The Lazy Way

REPLACING THE PCV VALVES AND FILTERS

The positive crankcase ventilation (PCV) valve and filter must be replaced each year or every 15,000 miles if you want your car to run properly. Replacing these things is not hard, and it takes just a few minutes if you follow these easy steps:

1. Locate the air filter housing and element.

2. Remove the lock nut that holds the housing and air filter.

3. Twist the PCV valve away from the rubber grommet in the valve cover without tearing or forcing.

4. Check the hose to the PCV valve for cracks.

5. Lift out the old PCV filter and replace it with a new one.

6. Reinstall the air filter and housing cover.

7. Attach the new PCV valve to the hose and twist it into the grommet on the valve cover.

EMISSIONS CHECKS

Your car is designed to control the emissions of a wide range of noxious chemicals, including hydrocarbons, nitrogen oxides, and carbon monoxide. There are three types of controls on your car to handle these gases: engine modifications, external cleaning systems, and fuel system vapor controls. When these controls are well-maintained, they do a very good job of reducing harmful

YOU'LL THANK YOURSELF LATER

It's against federal and state law to remove or disable any emission control device. Don't alter, disconnect, or override emission controls for any reason.

exhaust emissions. Most states have some type of requirements about emissions inspections as part of the regular yearly state inspections. It's best to have your mechanic take care of these problems.

STATE SAFETY INSPECTIONS

Most states require that you schlep your car into a state inspection center to be inspected each year, to make sure your car isn't going to cause some sort of safety problem out on the road. Just because your car passes an inspection, it does not mean that your car is perfect in every way. Some owners have a false sense of security after an inspection and figure that they don't have to worry about their car for the next six months.

Requirements for state inspections vary according to locality, but most inspectors check things such as windshield wipers, lights, front end and steering, suspension, turn signals, tires, brakes, and the exhaust system. Stuff on your car that doesn't directly affect safety, such as a radiator leak, won't be checked. However, a good technician will let you know if he or she notices other problems.

QUICK ■ PAINLESS

Get a list of your state's inspection criteria and follow the guidelines. Keep your sticker up to date, but do your part. An inspection isn't a complete tune-up and overhaul.

Getting Time on Your Side

	The Old Way	The Lazy Way
Fixing hole in the tailpipe	1 hour	15 minutes
Troubleshooting the exhaust system	Uh oh!	15 minutes
Replacing an exhaust pipe	2 hours	30 minutes
Replacing the PCV valves and filter	2 hours	20 minutes
Making do if the muffler falls off on the road	Uh oh!	10 minutes
Keeping your car road-legal	Uh oh!	20 minutes a month

Simply Steering Through Trouble

Back when Henry Ford was putting together his assembly line, cars were a lot simpler than they are today. Steering systems, for example, were rudimentary. As years went on, the cars grew larger and heavier, and their steering systems began to incorporate modern technological advances.

More and bigger cars led to more and bigger roads and faster speeds. With the development of modern superhighways came the need to control the cars flying along at high speeds with steering that could respond instantly to the driver's movements. Power steering mechanisms enabled drivers to do just that.

When your wheels aren't going in the same direction as your steering wheel, you've got big problems, and you're going to have to do something about it. But odds are you don't have the tools, the training, or the time to fix the steering. So read on to find out the least you need to know about

Forewarned is forearmed! Make sure you understand how your car steers and protect yourself!

your steering system, what things you can do to keep it running, and when you should just take it in and let the professionals have a look.

HOW STEERING WORKS

When you rotate the steering wheel of your car, it turns a steering gear, which is connected to rods and joints; these rods and joints are attached to the front wheels. Your car will have either rack-and-pinion steering or recirculating ball steering; both of these systems can be found in either manual or power steering.

Power Steering

If you had to turn the wheels simply by manually turning the steering wheel alone, it would take lots of strength. Instead, a power boost to the steering, just like with the brakes, allows you to steer the car much more easily. When the engine starts, a belt-driven pump on the engine sends pressurized hydraulic fluid through high-pressure hoses to the steering gear box, where a piston is connected to the steering linkage. When you turn the steering wheel, high-pressure oil flows into the piston, which helps you turn the wheel. Low-pressure oil returns to the steering pump reservoir through a return hose.

There are two kinds of power steering systems: variable assist and variable ratio. Many cars today combine both systems into a single power-steering unit.

Variable Assist

If you like to be able to have a sense of the road you're driving on, especially around curves, then variable assist steering will help you to do that. You get this feel for the road because how the hydraulic pressure acts on the pistons varies depending on the driving conditions. This process gives you a feel for the road based on how much effort you put into driving.

For example, if you must whip the wheel sharply to the left or right to avoid a deer bounding into your road, you put more force on the control valve in the power steering mechanism, and the system assists your steering more. However, if you're simply steering gently around a curve or driving straight down a road, the power steering system doesn't provide you with much extra assistance, so it feels more as though you're controlling the steering wheel. Driving down a straight road provides almost no assist, so slight corrections you need to make provide you with a good sense of control and of being in touch with the road surface.

Variable Ratio

With variable ratio steering, you don't have to turn the wheel so often when you're parking, and steering isn't as sensitive when you are driving in a straight line. A special design of the gear teeth in the steering gear box provides for variable ratio steering.

Rack-and-Pinion Steering

Most new cars have rack-and-pinion steering, a type of steering system that offers fast response. It includes a pinion gear that meshes with a steel bar (the rack) inside a housing, which is mounted parallel to the front axle.

Congratulations! You've learned about your steering system! Now kick back with the paper and enjoy the afternoon!

The Lazy Way

When you turn the steering wheel, the pinion gear also turns, making the rack slide inside its housing and moving the front wheels. The two ends of the rack are linked to the front wheels through tie rods, and the pinion gear is meshed to the rack. When the gear turns, the rack slides and moves the tie rods; the movement of the tie rods moves the wheels.

Recirculating Ball Steering

If you're driving a larger car or truck, you probably have a recirculating ball steering system, which features a gear box and more complex steering linkage. When you turn the steering wheel, it rotates a gear with a sort of rounded spiral grove in the steering gear box. A ball nut fits over this gear, and ball bearings are located between the gear and the ball nut. As you turn the steering wheel, the ball bearings move the ball nut, which rotates a shaft connected to the front wheels.

IDENTIFYING STEERING PROBLEMS

If you're driving down the road and suddenly find it difficult to steer, you need to track down the problem before something more serious occurs. For lazy car owners who don't have lots of time to waste on diagnosis, the following sections provide a quick rundown of what can go wrong with your steering.

Loss of Steering Power

If you suddenly find it hard to steer and you detect a sort of growling noise as you turn, it could be due to one of the following problems:

- The steering fluid might be low. You can fix this problem by adding fluid (as explained later in this chapter), but after you've done that, you need to visit the repair shop to find out what happened to the fluid you had.

- The front tire pressure might be too low, causing too much friction when you turn the wheel.

- The power assist unit may not be working.

- Your wheels may be out of alignment. (See Chapter 6.)

- The drive belt that runs to the pump may be broken.

Pulling

If you have to wrestle with your car's steering wheel like Hulk Hogan on a bad day, it could be caused by one of several problems:

- Loose steering linkage
- Worn steering mechanism
- Poor wheel alignment
- Unevenly inflated tires
- Brake problem
- Manufacturing defects in tires

Corner Sway

A loose or broken sway bar can make your car lean and sway when you turn a corner. Worn bushings can also make your car act like this on a turn. Take the car to your mechanic and have it checked out.

IF YOU'RE SO
INCLINED

To check your steering, drive on a flat, level road while holding the steering wheel lightly between your fingertips. The car should not drift to the left or right.

Shimmy

If whenever your tires meet a bump in the road you feel the back-and-forth wiggle in the steering wheel, that's shimmy. It could be caused by any of the following problems:

- Worn tie rods
- Wheel imbalance (if shimmy comes and goes at certain speeds)
- Loose wheel bearings
- Worn steering linkage parts (if the shimmy is induced during road bumps)
- Worn ball joints

Noises

As you turn the wheel, if your car starts whining and complaining more than a toddler at naptime, your car could have one of these problems:

- Cold power steering fluid that isn't flowing smoothly through the system (if the noise occurs just when you start the car)
- Low power steering fluid level
- Defective power steering pump
- Loose or slipping belt on the power steering pump (this problem causes a high-pitched screech)

Smoke and Sulfur Odor

If your steering suddenly feels sluggish just as white smoke suddenly puffs out from under the hood and a smell of sulfur floods the air, you may well have a leak from the power steering fluid reservoir or hoses.

LOCATING A LEAK

If the level of your power steering fluid drops, you know you've got a leak. Some leaks are obvious, such as when you're driving down the road and smoke starts billowing out of the engine and oil covers the manifold when you look under the hood. Sometimes you may find puddles of fluid under the car. But other times, leaks are more subtle. Here's *The Lazy Way* to track down a power steering fluid leak:

1. Top off the power steering reservoir with fluid.

2. Clean any areas of the engine that may be covered in fluid.

3. Turn on the engine and let it idle.

4. Have a helper turn the wheel left and right a few times.

5. While the wheel is being turned, carefully check the following:

   - Power steering pump to high-pressure hose connection

   - High-pressure hose to steering box connection

   - Steering box to low-pressure hose connection

   - Low-pressure hose to pump connection

   - Remote reservoir (if your car has one) and hose connections

YOU'LL THANK YOURSELF LATER

Pinpoint your leaky hoses: a leaking high-pressure hose will squirt fluid everywhere; a leaking low-pressure hose will drip fluid.

- Front shaft seal on the pump
- Junction between reservoir and pump
- Steering rack boots
- Seals in the steering box

CHECKING YOUR STEERING SYSTEM

To save time at a repair shop later on, here are a few things you can check on your steering system:

1. Check periodically (every 1-2 months) for torn rubber boots on the steering rack where the rods are connected. The boots keep debris from building up on the rack.

2. Check all four CV joint boots on front-wheel drive cars at the same time.

3. Check tie rod and other steering joint boots for road debris, which is abrasive. Check for damaged boots. Lubricant can be washed out, causing premature wear.

4. Check for excessive play in the CV joint by pushing or pulling it while the car is raised off the ground on a ramp or jack stand.

Checking Power Steering Fluid

It's not hard to check power steering fluid if you suspect you're running low:

1. Locate the power steering reservoir.

2. Turn the reservoir lid counterclockwise (the dipstick is connected to the lid).

3. Wipe off the dipstick and insert it back in the reservoir.

4. Remove the dipstick and read the level marked on the dipstick.

5. If you need to add fluid, check your owner's manual for the type of fluid and specific instructions. (Some cars require a particular type of power steering fluid whereas others stipulate you use automatic transmission fluid.)

Filling Power Steering Fluid

If your power steering reservoir is low, you'll have to add more fluid to make sure your power steering doesn't suffer.

Adding Power Steering Fluid

Here's what you'll need:

Clean cloth

Power steering fluid or automatic transmission fluid (check manual or reservoir cap for type of fluid required)

1 Locate the power steering reservoir.

2 Turn the reservoir lid counterclockwise (the dipstick is connected to the lid). Check the fluid level.

3 Add fluid to recommended level.

4 Replace the reservoir cover.

> **Congratulations! You've just filled your power steering reservoir. Now take a break and go take a dip in the pool.**
>
> *The Lazy Way*

SIMPLY STEERING THROUGH TROUBLE

Getting Time on Your Side

	The Old Way	The Lazy Way
Locating power steering leak	30 minutes	20 minutes
Diagnosing a steering problem	Hours	30 minutes
Finding the problem	30 minutes	20 minutes
Checking your CV joints	30 minutes	10 minutes
Fixing power steering leak	20 minutes	10 minutes

Bumps R Us: Heading Off Suspension System Problems

When you're flying down the road in your best imitation of Mario Andretti taking Mr. Toad's Wild Ride, the reason why you don't go flying off the road and sailing into space is because of your suspension, which suspends the chassis, power train, and body of the car. Your car's shock absorbers (shocks) and struts are what help your car hug the road. They also help protect you from every bump along the way.

Shocks and struts do more than just let you ride as if you're on a cushion of air, however. They let you fall into a pothole and come out the other side without bottoming out, and they control the action of your car's springs so you don't get whiplash every time you bounce down the road.

HOW SUSPENSION WORKS

High-performance cars often have hard suspension, which provides maximum cornering power at high speeds but not much of a comfortable ride. Soft suspension is often built into luxury cars and features a fantastic ride but not-so-hot cornering ability. Most suspension systems for average cars fall somewhere in between these two extremes, balancing performance with comfort.

Shocks

The job of the shocks is to control the boinging action of the car's springs. When you compress a spring and then let it go, it bounces up and down a number of times. If a car's springs weren't absorbed by the shocks, your car would bounce up and down just like an uncoiled spring every time you went over a bump—pretty uncomfortable!

A shock is made up of a tube filled with fluid surrounding a piston attached to a metal rod. When you drive through a pothole, oil is forced through valves in the piston as it moves up and down; because the oil can't be compressed, only a certain amount of this fluid can be pushed through the valves. The result is resistance to the car's movement. Most standard types of shocks use this hydraulic oil. Most cars have one shock absorber for each wheel, but off-road vehicles may add a few extra shock absorbers on each wheel.

When you're buying shocks to replace the ones you have, reach for top-shelf brands, such as the newer gas-filled shock absorbers. They're more expensive, but when it comes to your suspension, you really do get what you pay for. Gas-filled brands are better than regular hydraulic shock absorbers because the pressurized gas prevents bubbles from forming in the hydraulic fluid. These bubbles interfere with the ability of shocks to soften that bone-crunching bounce that you'd get otherwise. Expensive shocks also speed up the response of the shock absorber's movement, so you feel more comfortable and in control.

Self-leveling shocks use a valve to maintain normal curb height when you've stuffed your car with your son's Webelo den and all their camping gear. With this type of shocks, compressed air pumps up the shocks when necessary so that the suspension can handle the extra weight. The extra air can be removed for normal loads.

You can adjust adjustable shock absorbers for a hard or soft ride, depending on where you intend to drive.

Struts

Struts look like conventional shock absorbers, and they perform the same shock-absorbing function. If you've got a new car, odds are you now have struts, not shock absorbers. Although the idea behind struts is similar to the idea behind shocks, the springs are built in. Although struts are more compact than the old system, they're also more expensive to replace. If you drive a commercial truck or van, you can get heavy-duty shock absorbers and struts.

QUICK ⏣ PAINLESS

Get the facts on your shocks so you can ride comfortably!

IF YOU'RE SO
INCLINED

If your older car rides rough and the suspension has never been replaced, try new shock absorbers first. If that doesn't solve the problem, try new springs.

Springs

No matter what kind of suspension system your car has, it includes some type of springs to support the weight of the car. These springs may include the following:

- Coil springs are the most common type of spring and are wound around a cylindrical form.

- Leaf springs are one or more flat pieces of tempered steel.

- A torsion bar is a steel rod that can twist and untwist itself.

Front Suspension

The front suspension holds up the front part of your car, including the power train, and stabilizes it in turns and bumps. Most cars have independent suspensions, which means that either of the two wheels can react to bumps independently without affecting the other wheel. There are four types of suspensions:

- Double A arm: This type of suspension is often used on high-performance cars and some trucks. It gets its name from the shape of the two control arms on either side of your car that connect the chassis to the steering knuckle.

- Leaf spring: In this type of suspension, the springs are usually mounted lengthwise (although some-times they are mounted side to side). Four-wheel drive cars most often have this type of heavy-duty suspension spring. Most of the time, a leaf spring suspension isn't an independent suspension, so if one wheel hits a bump, the other wheel also reacts.

- Longitudinal torsion bar: Light trucks and four-wheel drive cars often use this type of independent front suspension, which features pivoting control arms that mount to the car's chassis. Torsion bars (not springs) are used to provide springing action. As the wheel moves up and down, the control arm twists the torsion bar, which resists the twist motion.

- McPherson struts: Once found only on foreign cars, this type of independent front suspension is now found on many American cars. It's dramatically different from other types of front suspensions, but it works pretty much the same. All the components are found in one assembly based on a triangle design, including a coil spring and a shock absorber. This assembly is located between the top arm of the steering knuckle and the inner fender panel.

Rear Suspension

The rear suspension has to support the rear of the car, thereby increasing stability and comfort. Although independent suspensions designs can be used in the rear as well, these designs don't have to deal with steering, so they aren't as complex as their cousins up front. There are three main types of rear suspensions:

- Coil spring suspension: These act just like the ones on the front, except they are mounted between the rear axle and chassis.

YOU'LL THANK YOURSELF LATER

Keep an eye on your suspension and protect yourself from a bad situation later on!

■ Leaf spring suspension: If you have a rear-wheel drive suspension system, the leaf springs are attached to a frame or a subframe and help move the car and support the differential.

■ Transversely mounted torsion bar: Found mostly on small front-wheel drive cars, this type of torsion bar is much like the torsion bar on a front suspension. The rear bar works the same way, but it is mounted across the rear of the car from side to side.

Electronic Suspension

Some cars may also have electronically controlled shock absorbers or struts, which can be altered to account for road conditions and driving style. These systems can even lower the car to the ground at higher speeds to boost gas mileage; as the car slows down, the car rises again.

CHECKING FOR WORN SHOCKS AND STRUTS

Just like everything else in life, your shocks and struts will gradually wear out over time. Unfortunately, you can't fix a worn-out shock; all you can do is put in a new one.

How fast your own particular car goes through a set of shocks and struts depends on how and where you drive. If you live in a city and pick your way slowly and carefully along ruler-straight roads and never skirt anywhere near a pothole, your system will last much longer than the Evel Knievel who drives like mad over roads that resemble the surface of the moon.

As dirt, gravel, ice, and other road objects are kicked up from the road, they can nick the piston rod, which can in turn damage the piston seal. When this happens, fluid starts to leak from the seal; eventually, the shock loses its ability to function, just like you would if you cut an artery and didn't put on a bandage. The effects of rough roads and tough driving are amplified if your chassis parts are worn. Such conditions cause joints and rubber parts to wear out faster.

Does Your Suspension Pass the Test?

There's a fast, easy way to test how well your car's suspension system is functioning without driving into your repair shop. Take this lazy quiz to find out:

1. Do you hit your head on the ceiling every time your car takes a dip?

   ☐ Yes ☐ No

2. Does your car bounce excessively (three or more times) when you drive through an intersection or over a dip?

   ☐ Yes ☐ No

3. If you push down hard on the hood, does the car bounce up and down like a cork in the ocean? (It should only bounce once.)

   ☐ Yes ☐ No

4. When you slam on the brakes, does your car rock back and forth?

   ☐ Yes ☐ No

YOU'LL THANK YOURSELF LATER

It's easy to see a leak from shocks and struts: The fluid runs down the housing, and road dirt will stick to it.

QUICK ◼️ PAINLESS

Be sure the car is parked on a stable base (a garage floor or 2-foot squares of plywood) when you use jack stands.

5. When you apply the brakes at high speed, does the car drift left or right?

☐ Yes   ☐ No

6. When you change lanes to get around that dolt in the '62 Buick, does your car sway from side to side like a hammock in the breeze?

☐ Yes   ☐ No

7. If you're driving on the off ramp at the turnpike, does your car lean and sway so much that you feel out of control?

☐ Yes   ☐ No

8. If you look at your car head-on from a few feet away, does it sag to one side?

☐ Yes   ☐ No

If you answer yes to any of these questions, your suspension fails the test. Take your car in for a suspension check-up.

Checking Out the Suspension

From your answers to the quiz, you've figured out whether you may have a problem. Now you can take a look yourself. It only takes a few minutes, and it beats driving all the way to the repair shop only to be told you're worrying over nothing. To conduct a visual inspection, you're going to need to scrunch under your car, so you'll need to raise the car up onto jack stands.

1. Put a chock behind the rear wheels.

2. Raise one front wheel with the jack and place a safety stand under a solid mounting point. Lower the car onto the jack stand.

3. Raise the other front wheel with the jack, and place a safety stand under it in a matching spot. Lower the car onto the jack stand.

4. Slide under the car and look at each wheel's spring and shock absorber for the following items:

   - A properly seated spring
   - Cracks or obvious deformities of the coil
   - Dents, cracks, or leaks in the shock absorbers
   - Loose or missing mount bolts in the shock absorber mounting points

5. Tighten loose bolts.

6. Inspect all metal rods, links, bushings, and arms.

7. Grip the wheel at top and bottom and try to wiggle it to check for play in bearings and joints. Grip the wheel at front and rear and repeat the process. There shouldn't be much play, if any at all.

8. Spin the wheel and listen for wheel bearing noise (growling sound) on rear-wheel drive cars. On front-wheel drive cars, you can spin the rear wheels and listen for bad wheel bearings.

9. Lower the car and repeat the process with the rear suspension.

Congratulations! You've successfully tested your suspension system. Now take a break and go listen to *Cartalk* on the radio.

The Lazy Way

Getting Time on Your Side

	The Old Way	**The Lazy Way**
Testing shocks	2 hours	5 minutes
Checking the suspension	2 hours	10 minutes
Finding out if you have a problem	Uh oh!	2 minutes
Finding a leak from your shocks	15 minutes	2 seconds
Checking your wheel bearings	Uh oh!	10 minutes
Understanding how your suspension works	"I'll never get it!"	15 minutes

Chapter sixteen

Cooling Off the Cooling System

The cooling system is designed to keep your engine operating at the right temperature for optimum performance and to transfer heat away from the engine. When you realize that the temperature inside your engine is usually above 400 degrees Fahrenheit, you can see how important this job is. Most new cars have a pressurized system for cooling the engine that uses a thermostat to control how much coolant percolates through the engine. The system is pressurized so that it can run at a higher boiling point; but all of the parts, including hoses, must be tough enough to withstand all that pressure.

The water pump is the most important part of your cooling system, forcing the coolant through the engine block, heater core, and radiator. A little bit of seepage from the pump is normal, but cascading coolant means you've got a pump breakdown.

CHECKING YOUR COOLING SYSTEM

Of course, you've been checking the coolant in your system once a month (or at least every 3,000 miles) to make sure you won't overheat in summer or freeze in winter. But there's more you can do if you want to prevent problems with your cooling system down the road.

Check All Hoses

Because hoses spend their entire lives coping with pressure, odds are that sooner or later one might blow. For that reason, you should check your hoses once a month for swollen areas, worn spots, or loose clamps. Replace any hoses that are worn, cracked, partly split, or that feel mushy or brittle when you squeeze them.

To replace a hose, follow these steps:

1. Drain the cooling system by removing the radiator cap and loosening the small faucet on the inside of the lower tank of the radiator (the *petcock*) or removing the lower radiator hose.

2. Loosen the clamps and slide them out of the way.

3. Twist and pull off the old hose. If it's stuck, cut a four- or five-inch slit lengthwise from the end and use a screwdriver to pry it loose.

4. Clean all the metal connections with a wire brush.

5. Slip a new clamp on each end of the new hose.

6. Position the hose on the fittings.

7. Slide the clamps into position about an inch from the end of the hose, as close to the bead as possible,

and tighten the clamps. (But don't go crazy with your tightening; you could damage the hose!)

8. Refill the cooling system and replace the radiator cap.

9. Run the engine and check for leaks.

Keeping the Coolant Clean

Rust and scale that form in the engine should be flushed out to allow the engine to operate at peak efficiency. Even though the antifreeze might not be that old and the freeze protection still works, the coolant's antirust and lubricating additives will wear out. When antifreeze breaks down, corrosive acids start attacking the engine, and the next thing you know, you've got engine failure because of invisible internal coolant leaks.

Some experts recommend that you flush and refill the cooling system every two years or 24,000 miles, but you should really do this job once a year to be safe. You can tell it's time to flush the coolant if you see a murky or rusty liquid swirling around in the radiator.

Choosing a Coolant

Don't use recycled coolant. Standard coolant doesn't cost much, and when it's time to flush your system, standard coolant is what you should use. The truly lazy car owner might want to reach for the bright orange Dex-Cool, the latest in antifreeze technology. It only has to be flushed every five years (or 100,000 miles), which is more than

YOU'LL THANK YOURSELF LATER

Make sure the radiator cap seals are clean, flexible, and uncracked. If the cap doesn't seal properly, the cooling system won't function correctly.

twice the standard coolant's change interval. It's been a standard in General Motors' cars since the mid-1990s.

Some manufacturers have approved the use of propylene-based coolants because they are allegedly more environmentally friendly than regular coolant and won't poison your pets. However, propylene coolants have a higher viscosity than standard ethylene glycol and may interfere with the performance of your defroster and heater. These coolants also tend to freeze and boil over more quickly. Although some car makers have approved these coolants, others have not, so be warned that using a propylene-based coolant may invalidate your warranty.

FLUSHING THE COOLING SYSTEM

If you've looked into your radiator and seen something that looks rusty and dirty, it's probably time to flush the cooling system. If you live in a cold climate, it's best to flush the system in the fall before the blizzards hit. If you live in a year-round warm climate, it's just as important to get your cooling system ready for hot weather, when an unattended system could boil over. You should flush your coolant in the spring before hot weather sets in.

You have a choice of either flushing just the radiator or backflushing the entire system with the help of a flushing kit. (You can buy a kit at any auto parts store.) Backflushing means that you're reversing the normal direction of the coolant flow, which helps to flush away contaminants that clog the coolant's passageways. When you backflush, the old coolant is forced upward and out through the radiator neck. When you're finished flushing or backflushing, you will need to add more antifreeze. Make sure you have enough on hand.

Flushing or backflushing: which to choose? Either is an acceptable way for the lazy car owner; it's not as complicated to flush just the radiator, but using the kit isn't hard, and this way the entire system is cleaned. Check your owner's manual to see which method your car's manufacturer recommends.

Using a Kit to Backflush

If you use a kit, you'll get some plastic tee fittings in different sizes, one of which will fit your heater hose, where it will be permanently inserted.

Backflushing Your Coolant System

Here's what you'll need to backflush your system with a kit:

Flushing/filling kit
Screwdriver
Knife
Garden hose
Pliers
Coolant

1 Read the kit instructions.

2 Start with a cold engine.

3 Set heater controls on the dash to maximum so you can flush the heater core as well as the radiator and engine.

QUICK n PAINLESS

If you have a four-gallon cooling system and your antifreeze/water ratio is 50/50, you'll need to add two gallons of antifreeze to the radiator.

When you place a tee connection on your heater hose, you won't be taking it off; it will be there the next time you want to flush the system.

4 Find the heater hose that attaches to the cylinder head. If you have trouble finding the right hose, check your owner's manual.

5 Cut this hose at a point lower than the opening in the radiator neck. Don't panic; some coolant will leak out, but that's okay.

6 Put loose hose clamps on each end of the cut hose, and then slide both ends of the hose onto the tee connection. Tighten clamps with a screwdriver.

7 Screw the adapter onto the tee and connect the garden hose to the top of the tee.

8 Remove the radiator cap.

9 Insert the radiator nozzle (it comes with the kit!) into the radiator. This nozzle will direct the old coolant that you're flushing up and out of the radiator. If the nozzle doesn't fit, don't be alarmed; the old coolant will just flow out of the radiator.

10 Turn on the spigot connected to the garden hose.

11 Water will enter the tee, flow through the cooling system, and come out the radiator opening.

12 When the water starts to flow, turn on the engine.

13 Flush the system until the water runs clear.

14 Turn off the water and the engine.

15 Drain the radiator by opening the handle of the petcock found on the bottom of the radiator tank. When the radiator is finished draining, close the petcock tightly. (If there's no petcock, disconnect the lower radiator hoses; connect them again after draining the radiator.)

16 Still keeping the cap off the flushing tee, slowly add the correct amount of antifreeze for your climate. Because antifreeze is heavier than water, it will sink to the bottom and push out any clean water left in the bottom of the system. As you pour in the antifreeze, you'll see this clean water seeping out from the flushing tee.

17 When you've reached the right amount of water and antifreeze, cap the flushing tee with the plastic cap from your kit.

18 Replace the radiator cap.

Removing Air Bubbles

Some newer front-wheel drive cars are built with a heater core that's higher than the radiator neck. This means that when you refill the system up to the radiator neck, there's an air pocket in the heater core, which can lead to overheating. To remove this air pocket, follow these steps:

1. Raise the front end of the car, either with a ramp or jack/jack stand.

2. Take off the radiator cap.

IF YOU'RE SO
INCLINED

You can premix coolant by emptying half a gallon of antifreeze into another clean, empty one gallon container. Fill each container with half a gallon of clean water; you now have two gallons of 50/50 antifreeze/water.

3. Turn on the heater controls to maximum to open the heater valve.

4. Run engine for five minutes in park or neutral.

5. After five minutes, shut off the engine.

6. Check the coolant level in the radiator. You may need to add more water.

7. Replace the radiator cap.

Flushing the Radiator

If you don't want to end up on the side of the road with a radiator spewing more steam than Old Faithful, you'll admit that no matter how pressed for time you are, you can spare a few moments once a year to flush your radiator.

The Big Flush

Here's what you'll need to flush the radiator:

Dishpan to catch old antifreeze
Garden hose
Owner's manual
Antifreeze tester
Antifreeze

1 Place the dishpan under the radiator.

2 To drain the old antifreeze, open the small faucet on the inside of the lower tank of the radiator (petcock) or remove the lower radiator hose. Fluid will drain into the dishpan.

3 Dispose of antifreeze according to container instructions. (Remember: antifreeze is poisonous!)

4 Remove the radiator cap.

5 When the radiator is empty, insert a garden hose into the radiator, turn on the water, and let water run through the radiator until it drains clear.

6 Turn off the water and close the petcock (or reinstall the lower radiator hose).

7 Read your owner's manual to find out how much coolant your car will hold.

8 Add the proper amount of antifreeze to the radiator.

9 Add water to the radiator until it is full and replace the radiator cap.

10 Run engine for a few minutes until the thermostat opens fully. The top and bottom radiator hoses will feel hot to the touch.

11 Recheck the coolant level. If liquid is not up to the radiator neck, add more coolant when the engine cools down.

AIR CONDITIONING SYSTEM

Don't even think about servicing your air conditioning system unless you're a well-trained mechanic familiar with proper safety procedures, the use of necessary special equipment, and regulations governing the evacuation, recovery, and disposal of toxic automotive refrigerants. The refrigerant is extremely cold when

> Congratulations! You've just flushed your coolant system. Now go take a swing in the hammock and have some lemonade.

The Lazy Way

Use protective goggles and rubber gloves when dealing with dangerous fluids!

compressed, and when it is released into the air, it will instantly freeze anything it contacts—including your eyes. If that hasn't convinced you, remember that the refrigerant becomes a deadly poisonous gas in the presence of an open flame; one good whiff of vapors from burning refrigerant can be fatal.

Getting Time on Your Side

	The Old Way	The Lazy Way
Adding coolant	Every year	Every 5 years
Flushing the system	1 hour	30 minutes
Checking the system	2 hours	15 minutes
Replacing a hose	1 hour	20 minutes
Flushing the radiator	1 hour	20 minutes
Removing air bubbles	1 hour	20 minutes

Chapter seventeen

Fendering Off Trouble: Handling Highway Hazards

Did you ever notice you never run out of gas when you're sitting smack next door to an Exxon station? That's because life's little annoying emergencies usually occur when you're in the middle of Montana without a cell phone. Because life's like that, odds are you've probably already joined an auto club to bail you out when you run out of gas or have a flat. For that occasional lapse, the club can be a real lifesaver.

But there are other times when it simply pays to know how to get yourself out of a sticky auto situation. For example, if you get stuck in a blizzard, odds are you're not going to be first on the list when your auto club comes to pull you out. In times of severe weather, you may have to cool your tires for several hours at the side of the road. For those of us without

much time to waste, it pays to learn how to take care of your own car emergencies.

WINTERIZING

Before we get into how to handle highway hazards once they occur, the lazy car owner can save lots of time by being prepared. If it gets cold and snowy where you drive, you're going to need to get ready for those inevitable blizzard conditions:

1. Change the oil and filter according to your manual's recommendations.

2. Make sure your coolant is 50/50 water and antifreeze, which will protect your car even below zero. If the coolant is more than two years old (or you've driven beyond 24,000 miles) you should flush the coolant (see Chapter 16). In very cold climates, mix the antifreeze to the specifications on the container.

3. Check for frays, cracks, and aging areas on hoses and drive belts. Replace any hoses or belts that are four years old or older.

4. Clean/check battery cables and water level; check battery condition and charging level.

5. Check fluid levels, and add antifreeze to your windshield washer solvent.

6. If you have a newer car, have your annual emission tune-up and replace spark plugs if necessary.

7. Check tires for damage and make sure they're properly inflated. Replace worn tires, and put on snow tires or good quality all-season tires.

8. Check all lights and signals.

9. Replace wiper blades.

10. Get your brakes inspected.

11. Lubricate all weather stripping and door and trunk locks with spray lubricant.

12. Make sure your heater and defroster work.

13. Check the fuel filter in the fall and remove any built-up water (especially in diesel cars).

14. If you have a diesel car, check the glow plug operation.

15. Consider adding gasoline antifreeze ("dry gas") if you live in a very cold climate to prevent gas lines from freezing.

K-RATIONS FOR YOUR CAR

If you keep an old duffel bag full of emergency supplies in your trunk, you won't have to waste time and energy walking to the nearest auto supply store two miles away when you break down. Here's what you'll need:

- Battery jumper cables
- First aid kit
- Large flashlight/extra batteries
- Emergency flares

Congratulations! You've winterized your car! Now go hop in your hot tub and forget the cold weather!

The Lazy Way

- Small shovel
- Blanket
- Funnel
- Bag of cat litter
- Nonperishable food
- Plastic jug of water
- Empty emergency gas can
- Rubber hammer
- Wheel chock
- Work gloves
- Small tool kit
- Spray can of penetrating oil (WD-40)
- Four-way tire wrench
- Duct tape
- Spare fuses

Add the following items to your emergency stash in the trunk in the beginning of winter if you live in a cold, snowy climate:

- Spare gloves, boots, jacket, blanket, overalls
- Tire chains
- Windshield scraper/brush
- Candles, matches
- Moisture-displacing spray lubricant

Now that you have your emergency kit together, you can relax knowing that you're prepared should anything happen. And when it does…

IF YOU'RE SO
INCLINED

Not everyone can afford a cellular phone, but try hard to work this item into your budget. With a cell phone, you can call for help without leaving your car, report others' emergency situations, notify your boss you'll be late, or order a pizza. It's the ultimate lazy person's weapon.

SAFETY FIRST!

If you find yourself broken down on the side of the road, keep these safety guidelines in mind:

1. Pull the car completely off the road.

2. Don't stand near the highway when checking the car.

3. In the daytime, raise the hood and tie a white scarf to the antenna. In the nighttime, turn on your emergency flashers.

4. Set out flares behind and in front of your car.

5. If you can't fix the car yourself, stay inside with the windows up and the door locked. Never accept a ride from another motorist.

QUICK **n'** PAINLESS

Keep some flares in the car in case you ever break down at night so that other motorists can see you

FIXING A FLAT IN NO TIME FLAT

Of course your tire will deflate at the world's most inopportune time. Your choice: wait for the auto club or change it yourself. When you hear that characteristic thump! thump!, drive as far onto the shoulder as you can. Try to find the most level spot, because if you park on a slope, you risk having the car roll off the jack. If you drive very far on a flat tire, you'll ruin both the tire and the wheel, so try to find the first flat spot available.

Remove the jack from the trunk and read all the instructions for setting up the jack, which should be printed on the trunk lid. Every car has a particular spot where the jack should be placed, and they aren't all the same. Like a fire drill, this is a good thing to practice.

Could you find what you need and change the tire? Is everything you need in the car? Try it!

Changing a Tire

Here's what you'll need to get the job done:

Tire jack equipment

Lug wrench

Screwdriver

Spare tire

1. Before jacking up the car, remove the hubcap with the screwdriver or lug wrench. (For alloy wheels, remove the lug nut cover.)

2. Loosen the lug nuts, using the weight of the car as leverage.

3. If the lug nuts won't budge, spray them with a bit of WD-40 oil that you've cleverly already packed into your emergency kit in the trunk.

4. Jack up the car according to your manual. Keep going until the tire is about two inches off the ground.

5. Take off the loosened lug nuts and the wheel. Drop the lug nuts into the hubcap, so you don't lose them in the weeds.

6. Put on the spare, replacing all the lug nuts and tightening them lightly with your finger.

7. Lower the car and completely tighten the lug nuts one by one with your lug wrench.

8. Replace the hubcap or lug nut cover and tap it into place with the rubber mallet from your emergency kit.

YOU'LL THANK YOURSELF LATER

If you've bought a used car, check to make sure the jack is the correct one for the model you purchased. Make sure there's a correct lug wrench, too.

9 Put the jack and flat tire back in the trunk.

10 Stop at the repair shop as soon as possible to fix the tire. If you're driving a space-saver spare, be sure you don't drive any faster than the warning recommendation printed on the tire.

11 Don't forget to fix the flat as soon as possible; remember, you no longer have a spare.

REVIVING A DEAD BATTERY

You drive to the park in the pouring rain, so you have your lights on. But when you get there, the sun comes out, and you forget to turn off the lights. Five hours later, you return to a car with a lifeless battery. If you don't want to wait for the auto club, you can jump it yourself, provided you can find your way around a battery and find somebody else to let you borrow his battery.

No matter how much you think you know about jumping batteries—and no matter how much the other guy insists he knows—before you start, read your manual. Some of the newer computer-controlled cars advise against jumping your car at all. If that's the case, then you'll have to wait for the experts. If the manual says it's okay to proceed, you'll need to snag a healthy battery.

In order to jump a battery, you'll need a car with a charged battery and a pair of jumper cables. If you've paid attention so far, you will have a pair of high-quality cables stowed in your emergency duffel in the trunk.

YOU'LL THANK YOURSELF LATER

Because your mechanic's air tool may inadvertently overtighten your lug nuts, always request that your lug nuts be hand-tightened to correct specifications whenever you take your car in for repairs that require wheel removal.

Now, here's what you do:

1. Park both cars facing each other or side by side with engines off, in as safe a position as possible.

2. Connect the red end of the cable to the positive battery terminal of the charged battery. The positive terminal is marked with a (+); it's usually larger.

3. Connect the other red end to the positive terminal of the dead battery.

4. Connect the black end of the cable to the negative terminal of the good battery.

5. Connect the other black end to the ground on the car with the dead battery. Use a heavy steel part for the ground (such as a bolthead or brace on the alternator).

6. Start the engine of the car with the good battery. Then start the engine in your car, and let both cars run for about five minutes.

7. Disconnect the negative cables first, starting with the ground. Then disconnect the positive jumper cables.

RUNNING ON EMPTY

You can avoid running out of gas if you make it a habit to always fill up when you're down to a quarter tank. It's truly *The Lazy Way* to avoid future hassles. However, if you're a gambler at heart or your gas gauge broke, you could end up at the side of the road with a long road to hike to the gas station. You thought you didn't have time to stop at the gas station? Do you have any idea how much more time it takes when you run out of gas?

Fortunately, you've been reading this book and know to keep an emergency empty gas can or a funnel in the trunk, so you'll have something to tote to the gas station to fill up. Those of you with old cars may have to pour a bit of gas directly into the carburetor to prime it (beware of backfires!). The new cars of today with fuel-injection systems or computer-controlled carburetors will start right up after you put the gas in the tank without being primed.

STUCK LIKE GLUE

Nothing is more frustrating than getting stuck in the snow when you're in a hurry. We've all seen those folks frantically rocking their car back and forth as they try to zoom their cars out of trouble. Usually, the only thing that happens when a motorist stands on the gas pedal out of sheer frustration is that the car just digs its way further down toward China. Rocking rarely works, and fierce rocking can do a great deal of damage to your car.

Whether you're stuck in sand, snow, or mud, if a bit of gentle rocking back and forth doesn't do the trick, you really have only two options: dig your way out or tow your way out. If you're opting for digging, get the little shovel that you've stowed in your trunk and dig your way into your wheels. Try laying down a bit of the kitty litter for traction, and slowly, gently back out of the mess. Some folks in snowy climates keep a pair of car

IF YOU'RE SO
INCLINED

Keeping a shovel and some kitty litter may seem like you're cramming your trunk full to overflowing, but these items will definitely get you out of a jam!

Congratulations! You've gotten your car out of the snowbank! Take a break and go curl up in front of the fire with a glass of milk and a bag of Oreos.

The Lazy Way

chains in the trunk; after you've dug your way to the back wheels, lay the chains under the wheel and carefully back out.

OUCH! IT'S HOT!

Overheating is the number-one cause of roadside breakdown. When the temperature soars and the traffic bogs down, overheating can become a real risk. It doesn't have to be. You can prevent overheating problems if your car tends in this direction. When you're driving in very hot weather and heavy traffic, try these tips:

1. Turn off the air conditioner and open the windows. Your grandparents drove without it, and you can, too. (Air conditioners put a heavy load on the engine and add to the heat.)

2. If the red warning light is still on, brace yourself and turn on the heater. This helps cool the car by sending coolant circulating to a larger area (for example, through the heater core).

3. When your car is idling in heavy traffic, put the car in neutral and step lightly on the gas pedal (but not too much). This action speeds up the fan and water pump, making the cooling system work better.

Overheating Treatment

If the previous tips don't work, it's time for some emergency intervention. When you notice steam pouring out from under the hood, you don't really have much of a choice but to pull over. You'll need:

Jug of water

Rag

Duct tape

1. Move off the road and allow the car to cool down (at least 20 minutes).

2. Place a rag over the radiator cap and press down hard, turning counterclockwise to the first notch.

3. After the initial pressure escapes, continue turning the cap until it comes off.

4. Start the car's engine and add water to the radiator.

5. Replace the radiator cap and lock it in place.

6. If a hose split due to overheating, wrap some duct tape from your emergency duffel around the hose.

7. As soon as possible, replace the lost coolant with the proper mix of antifreeze and water. Then figure out why the car is overheating!

LOCKED UP TIGHT

Nothing is nearly so frustrating as finding out you've locked your keys in the car. The best way to prevent this is to buy a small magnetized key holder and stick it under your car's fender. That way, you know you always have a spare key if you have a momentary lapse. If it's too late for that preventive tip, you have only a few options:

YOU'LL THANK YOURSELF LATER

Never add cold water to a hot engine; it could crack the engine block.

1. Call your auto club to bail you out or wait for a police officer (the police often have special tools to unlock a car).

2. Get the car dealer to make you another key. (They may need serial numbers on your locks or the numbers listed in your owner's manual.)

3. Get a ride home to fetch your spare keys.

4. In an emergency—say your infant is sitting in the back seat and it's a hot day—break the car window. Window replacement is very expensive, so don't use this option unless it's a matter of life or death.

COME BLOW YOUR HORN

If your car horn has ever been stuck on blare, you've probably thought about running and hiding—but stopping the noise isn't hard when you know where your horn is. It's a good idea to locate your horn when it's not going off, because you'll be a lot less rattled. Horns usually look sort of like a black snail, and they may be anywhere around the fender walls, behind the grille, or on the side of the radiator.

When you find it, all you have to do is pull its plug. If the horn is inaccessible, you can simply remove its fuse. Every car owner should learn where the fuse panel is. After you've done that, drive the car to the repair shop, so the mechanic can figure out what set off the horn in the first place.

QUICK ⬭ PAINLESS

If your car has a safety radiator cap with a lever to allow pressure to escape, cover the cap with a rag and open the lever; then remove the cap.

BRAKE LOSS

If you're careening down a hill and you realize your brakes are gone, panic is only a breath away. The only way you can handle this situation is to stay calm and try these remedies:

1. Pump the brake.

2. If that doesn't work, shift into second gear and then first. (Your car should slow down.)

3. Gently apply the parking brake.

4. If you're still moving and you're going to hit something, try to sideswipe a curb. (An indirect hit is always better than a direct hit.)

5. Don't turn the engine off, whatever you do. Your steering may lock up.

A COMPLETE WASTE OF TIME

The 3 Worst Things to Do when You Have Brake Problems:

1. Ignore soft, mushy brakes.

2. Ignore brakes that pull to one side.

3. Ignore a flashing brake dash light.

Getting Time on Your Side

	The Old Way	The Lazy Way
Fixing a flat tire	3 hours	30 minutes
Running out of gas (getting help)	2 hours	20 minutes
Getting Unstuck	30 minutes	15 minutes
Reviving a dead battery	Hours	10 minutes
Overheating your car	All summer long	Never again!
Getting locked out	Once a month	Never again!

More Lazy Stuff

How to Get Someone Else to Do It

Although you can do many car maintenance jobs yourself, most of your car's repairs should be done by professionals trained to handle today's complex machines. As in any profession, there are some dishonest mechanics, just like there are some dishonest lawyers, doctors, and bankers. But odds are your mechanic is a highly trained specialist who is acutely aware that your life could depend on how well he or she services your car. Auto technicians have families, too, and they don't want you out there on the road with your kids in the car, riding around on bald tires and faulty brakes.

Unfortunately, there is a persistent misconception that auto technicians are grease monkeys with an attitude who are out to rob you blind. This attitude is aided and abetted by local TV stations around the country who seem to delight in running "undercover" consumer sting operations in which they sabotage an engine and then film 10 poor sods trying to figure out what's wrong. Most shops today are staffed by honest, hardworking, and highly trained professionals who aren't trying to rip you off. If you choose your shop carefully, there's every reason to believe that you'll find an excellent repair person to take care of the things you're not qualified to do.

CHOOSING A SHOP

You wouldn't choose a heart surgeon by throwing a dart at the Yellow Pages, and you shouldn't pick your repair person because the shop is next door. Take a few minutes now to do some research, and you won't have to worry the next time your car needs to go in for repairs.

ASE Certification

One of the best ways to separate the wheat from the chaff when it comes to auto technicians is to look for ASE certification. The National Institute for Automotive Service Excellence (ASE) was started in the late 1960s when Congress was investigating charges of fraud in the auto repair industry. They didn't find much fraud, but they did uncover scads of incompetent mechanics, because at that time anybody with a toolbox could call himself or herself an auto technician. As a result, the ASE Institute began offering 32 tests in eight-test series for certification; today, more than 400,000 technicians are certified by ASE. A master auto technician has completed all the tests in his or her field.

Shopping Tips

Here's what you should do when looking for a good shop:

1. Call the Better Business Bureau or your state's Attorney General's office to see whether you can find a complaint about a shop.

2. Ask friends, family, and coworkers for details about a good person.

3. Visit the shop before taking in your car. Is the shop clean and well-organized? Are the employees clean, neat, and courteous? Are they the type of people you can communicate with?

4. Check for ASE certification or other specialized training.

5. Ask about how the shop determines prices for repairs.

6. Ask about the kind of diagnostic equipment the shop uses. Do the mechanics have access to computerized information? Do they have experience with your type of car?

7. Ask about the shop's guarantees.

8. Find out what recourse you have if you're not happy.

9. Ask about the possibility of a loaner car if yours isn't done in time.

10. Look over the cars that are on the lot or in the service bays. If they're all Yugos or 20-year-old heaps, you may not want to leave your BMW with this shop.

WHAT KIND OF SHOP IS THIS?

If you had a toothache, you wouldn't go to a urologist to have it pulled—at least, we hope you wouldn't. You shouldn't pull into a muffler shop for a rebuilt engine, either. Pick the right shop for the right job and the right mechanic for the right car.

New Car Dealer Service Department

Dealer service departments specialize in the kind of cars that the particular dealer sells, which means that they will have the most up-to-date information and equipment and parts to service the type of cars they sell. In addition, their auto technicians should all have the most recent factory training on those types of cars. If you have a really difficult problem, the dealer has access to factory service representatives that they can call upon for assistance. Of course, as long as your car is under warranty, you should take it to a dealer for service.

So why doesn't everyone patronize dealer service departments? First of all, they tend to be more expensive, which is why many people move on to independent shops after their warranties expire. In addition, most dealers pay their mechanics on a flat-rate system, so the mechanics are pressed to push their work through more rapidly. (In a flat-rate system, mechanics are paid a certain amount to do a job regardless of how long it takes them. The faster they do the job, the better opportunity they have to make more money, so they have more incentive to hurry.)

Independent Shops

Independent shops aren't affiliated with any particular dealer. They either perform general repairs on all cars or specialize in a particular type of car. The general repair shops are the jacks-of-all-trades in the car business; they'll work on any car that limps through the door, from basic American to exotic imports. Specialized independent shops focus on one brand or type of car, for example, German imports.

Many people find that smaller independent shops are less pressed for time and thus have more time to spend figuring out your car's problem. They may not work on flat rate, so you can be sure that the technician takes enough time to do the work properly. You may be able to more readily establish a rapport or line of communication. Just like in any other service job, you want to be able to talk to the expert and be understood.

Gas Stations

If you're driving along in an unfamiliar town and your tire blows, you can drive to a gas station for small repairs. Gas stations typically have one or two lifts for treating minor problems such as oil changes, tire rotations, inspections, and so on. They're not a bad choice for emergencies or for simple, basic jobs such as changing the oil or tires.

Specialty Repairs

Specialty repair shops hone in on one part of the car, such as the muffler, tires, or transmission. The shops could be owned either independently or franchised. Be wary of something that seems too good to be true, such as something that's very inexpensive and has a lifetime guarantee.

Tire Stores

If it's tires you want, you can go to a tire store and get not just tires but also repairs linked to tires (such as front-end alignments). Originally owned by large tire corporations as a way of selling tires, today tire stores may also perform other more general repairs. Quality here can vary, but they are a good place to get tires.

Quickie Service

What could please a lazy car owner more than an oil change in 10 minutes? Although saving time is a good idea, some of these zippy places don't hire the most experienced folks. When all the emphasis is placed on speed, quality can suffer. If a technician here notices another problem when he's got your car up on a lift, he may not have the time or inclination to mention it.

HOW TO RECOGNIZE A GREAT MECHANIC

You have a better chance of talking to the mechanic who works on your car at a smaller shop. In a larger shop, you may have to deal with the service writer who takes down your complaints and is the shop's liaison between the customer and employees.

Here's what you can expect from a good mechanic:

- Doesn't object to giving you an explanation about why parts were replaced. Don't be afraid to ask questions or ask the mechanic to save the old parts so you can look at them.

- Has ASE certification or other specialized accredited training.

- Has a clean work station with organized tools.

- Appears to have the right equipment and know-how to use it.

IT'S A TWO-WAY STREET

When you've found the dream shop and auto technician, you've got to do your part. Here's a mechanic's vision of a dream client:

- Arrive on time for your appointments.

- Try to be accurate and descriptive when explaining the problem.

- Leave the mechanic enough time to get the job done. If you're not waiting at the shop for the job to be completed, leave a number where you can be contacted if there are problems or you want to know what's going on.

- Let the mechanic do all the work on your car. Shops don't appreciate it if you bring your car in with an obscure problem that's hard to diagnose, but then you take the more profitable jobs (such as oil changes or brake work) down the road to a quickie place.

- If the mechanic seems to be reasonably competent, let him or her get on with his or her work without interruption. You don't want someone looking over your shoulder while you do your job, and neither does a mechanic.

- If you have a problem after your car has been worked on, return to the same shop and assume it was an honest error and that the problem can be resolved pleasantly. Don't automatically assume you're being ripped off.

- If the shop has fixed the stuck door handle on your 150,000-mile car and your starter breaks the next day, don't assume that the problem is the mechanic's fault. "It was working when I brought it in" is one of the most commonly heard complaints in a shop. Coincidences do happen, especially in an older car.

- If you went to see your doctor with vague health complaints and he or she couldn't diagnose your condition on the first visit, would you refuse to pay your bill? You'd be surprised how many customers expect perfect diagnoses each time they bring in a car.

- Pay your bill promptly.

If You Really Want More, Read These

Barbarossa, Fred and Saverio G. Bono. *The Car Care Book* (2nd ed.). Albany, NY: Delmar Publishers, 1988.

Cerullo, Bob. *What's Wrong With My Car?* New York: Plume Books, 1993.

Creative Homeowner Press. *Auto Cooling Systems How-To Booklet #510.* Upper Saddle River, NJ: Creative Homeowner Press.

Creative Homeowner Press. *Automotive Tools How-To Booklet #535.* Upper Saddle River, NJ: Creative Homeowner Press.

Creative Homeowner Press. *The Charging System How-To Booklet #507.* Upper Saddle River, NJ: Creative Homeowner Press.

Creative Homeowner Press. *CV Joints How-To Booklet #534.* Upper Saddle River, NJ: Creative Homeowner Press.

Creative Homeowner Press. *Drive-Train Service How-To Booklet #536.* Upper Saddle River, NJ: Creative Homeowner Press.

Creative Homeowner Press. *Engine Tune-up Basics How-To Booklet #509.* Upper Saddle River, NJ: Creative Homeowner Press.

Creative Homeowner Press. *Oil and Filter Changes How-To Booklet #501*. Upper Saddle River, NJ: Creative Homeowner Press.

Creative Homeowner Press. *Water Pumps How-To Booklet #529*. Upper Saddle River, NJ: Creative Homeowner Press.

Creative Homeowner Press. *Wiring and Lighting How-To Booklet #505*. Upper Saddle River, NJ: Creative Homeowner Press.

Fariello, Sal. *The People's Car Book: The One Essential Handbook for People Who Don't Trust Mechanics, Car Salesmen, or Car Manufacturers*. New York: St. Martin's Press, 1993.

Feirer, Mark. *The Family Handyman: Simple Car Care and Repair*. Pleasantville, NY: Reader's Digest Association, 1997.

Gaston, Jim. *Avoid Car Repair: Easy Ways to Keep Your Car Running Great*. Conation Publications, 1993.

———. *When There's No Mechanic: A General Guide to Driving, Maintenance, and Car Repair*. Conation Publications, 1992.

Gromer, Cliff (editor). *Popular Mechanics Saturday Mechanic*. New York: Hearst Books, 1994.

Havens, Gary (editor). *The Family Handyman: Simple Car Care and Repair*. Pleasantville, NY: Readers Digest Association, 1997.

Kline, David Nigel and Jamie Robertson. *All About Your Car*. DMI Press, 1997.

Magliozzi, Tom, Ray Magliozzi, and Harry Trumbore. *Car Talk*. New York: Dell Books, 1991.

Pete the Mechanic. "Understanding the Motor Oil Additive Package," *The Mechanic*. Winter 1996, 1, 4.

———. "A Leap Forward in Coolant Technology," *The Mechanic*. February 1997, 1, 2.

Newsom, Jim. "Normal, Everyday Driving Is Brutal," *The Mechanic*. February 1997.

Ramsey, Dan. *The Pocket Idiot's Guide to Car Repair*. New York: Alpha Books, 1997.

Schultz, Morth. *Car Care Q&A: The Auto Owner's Complete Problem Solver*. New York: John Wiley & Sons, 1992.

———. *Keep Your Car Running Practically Forever: An Easy Guide to Routine Care and Maintenance*. New York: Consumer Reports Books, 1991.

Schultz, Morth, Alfred W. Lees, and Ernest V. Heyn (editors). *What's Wrong with My Car? A Guide to Troubleshooting Common Mechanical and Performance Problems*. New York: Consumer Reports Books, 1990.

Stockel, Martin W., Martin T. Stockel, and Chris Johanson. *Auto Fundamentals*. Tinley Park, IL: The Goodheart-Willcox Co., Inc., 1996.

Treganowan, Lucille, and Gina Catanzarite. *Lucille's Car Care*. New York: Hyperion, 1996.

Volpe, Ren. *The Lady Mechanic's Total Car Care for the Clueless*. New York: St. Martin's Press, 1998.

If You Don't Know What It Means, Look Here

Accelerator   The gas pedal, used to control the car's speed.

Air cleaner   Plastic or metal housing that funnels air into the fuel delivery system. It contains the air filter.

Air filter   A paper filter in the air cleaner that prevents dust and dirt from getting into the engine.

Air pump   A device that pumps air into the exhaust manifold (and the catalytic converter) to cut down on the level of unburned fuel in the exhaust.

Alignment   Adjustments of the front wheels to make steering easier and provide optimum tire wear.

All-wheel drive   Much like four-wheel drive, this type of car has a small unit on the side of the transmission or inside the transmission that transmits power to all four wheels.

Alternator   Belt-driven power source that, when the car is running, electrically charges the battery and runs the electrical system.

Alternator belt   The belt that drives the alternator (the car's power source) and is connected at the crankshaft pulley.

Antifreeze   An ethylene glycol-based liquid that, when added to water in the radiator, keeps the car from freezing in winter and overheating in summer. Antifreeze and water are combined in a 50/50 mix that also helps to cut down on rust and corrosion.

Antilock brake system (ABS)   Computer-driven electronic braking system designed to shorten a car's stopping distance and prevent skids in emergency situations by controlling each wheel individually.

Automatic choke   A device that helps the engine start faster by increasing the richness of the fuel/air mixture. The device is operated by a thermostatic spring or other device that cuts air flow into a carburetor when the engine is cold.

Automatic transmission   A device that automatically selects and changes gears depending on the car's speed and load.

Automatic transmission fluid   A special type of light oil used in transmissions.

Axle   The metal shaft on which the wheels rotate.

Backflushing   Pumping a fluid in the opposite direction of the way it would normally go, as a way of cleaning the passages.

Ball joint   Similar to a human joint, the ball joint on a car is a ball and socket in the suspension that makes three-dimensional movement possible.

Battery   A device that produces and stores energy to provide direct current (DC) to power the starter, lights, and other electrical equipment by converting chemical energy into electrical energy. The battery is charged by the electricity-generating action of the alternator.

Battery terminals   The outside electrical connections of the battery found on the top or side of the device.

Bearings Small metal balls or rollers packed with grease that are designed to reduce friction between moving parts.

Blue book A weekly wholesale used car price guide (the Kelley Blue Book) published by the National Automotive Dealer Association.

Boot A pleated protective rubber or plastic cover that holds in grease in the CV joints in front-wheel drive cars or on steering racks to protect them from the elements.

Brake caliper The part in a disc brake system that squeezes brake pads against the disc, slowing down the car.

Brake drum A hollow metal part on a drum brake system that receives pressure from the semicircular brake shoes to slow and stop the car.

Brake fluid Fluid used in a hydraulic brake system.

Brake lines Reinforced rubber hoses (or metal tubes) carrying brake fluid between the master cylinder and wheel cylinder or brake calipers.

Brake lining A heat-resistant material attached to a disc brake pad or drum brake shoe.

Brake pad The flat replaceable surface of a disc brake system's calipers to which the disc brake lining is attached.

Brake shoes A crescent-shaped metal part to which the heat-resistant drum brake lining is attached.

Brake system The entire system that allows a car to slow and stop when you press the brake pedal. Pressing the brake pedal forces brake fluid through the master cylinder to hydraulic parts in the wheels; this action forces friction material against the rotor or drum. The brake system includes the brake pedal, linkage, master cylinder, brake lines, brake calipers, cylinders, and either a disc or drum brake at the wheel site.

Caliper   The part of a disc brake that presses on the pads, forcing them against the disc to slow or stop the car. Calipers can be movable or fixed in place.

Cam   A metal shaft projection that pushes against other moving parts as the shaft rotates.

Camber   Outward or inward angle of the top of a car's front wheels that is adjusted as part of an alignment to prevent tire wear.

Carbon monoxide   A colorless, odorless, tasteless, and highly poisonous gas produced by a car's exhaust system.

Carburetor   A device that atomizes gas with air so it can be distributed to the cylinders.

Caster   The forward or backward tilt of a car's front wheels that, when properly adjusted, provides a straight steer.

Catalytic converter   An emissions device much like a muffler that transforms harmful exhaust gases into fairly harmless nonpollutants emitted from the tailpipe.

Charging system   The electrical system that generates and stores electricity, including the alternator, voltage regulator, battery, and wiring system.

Chassis   The underlying frame of a car to which the power train and body are attached.

Chock   A small block of wood used to keep the car from rolling away while you're working on it.

Choke   A device that regulates the amount of air that enters the carburetor; when the choke is closed, the air/fuel mixture is richer, which helps a cold engine start and run.

Clutch   An assembly that can connect or disconnect the flow of torque between rotating parts.

Coil spring   A thick coiled steel bar that helps cushion bumps absorbed by the shock absorbers, helping to keep the car on an even keel.

Combustion   See combustion chamber.

Combustion chamber   The area at the top of a cylinder where the combustion of fuel and air occurs.

Compression ratio   A numerical comparison of a cylinder's cubic volume when a piston is at the top and bottom. The higher the compression ratio, the higher the octane rating of fuel that is required to prevent detonation problems while the car is running.

Connecting rods   Metal rods that connect the pistons to the crankshaft.

Coolant   A mixture of antifreeze and water in the car's cooling system that keeps the car from overheating in summer and freezing in winter; it also inhibits rusting and corrosion.

Cooling system   The system that stores and circulates coolant through the water jacket spaces in the engine head and block to prevent overheating.

Crankcase   The lower part of the engine block that houses the crankshaft and its surrounding parts. The car's oil pan is attached to the bottom of the crankcase.

Crankshaft   The primary rotating part of an engine, which supports the connecting rods and turns the up-and-down piston action into rotary motion.

CV joint   Constant velocity (CV) joints provide flexibility and are found at each end of the axles of front-wheel drive cars. They're covered by black accordion boots.

Cylinder   A tubular hollow area in the engine block in which a piston moves and where combustion takes place.

Cylinder head The metal section bolted on top of the engine block that forms part of the combustion chamber. It contains the intake and exhaust ports, valves, and threaded holes for the spark plugs.

Diesel engine An internal combustion engine that injects fuel oil directly into the cylinders. The high compression ratio creates such intense compression that the air itself is hot enough to ignite the diesel fuel without needing a spark.

Dieseling The condition (also called run on) in which a car keeps on running after the engine is turned off. The term refers to the fact that the engine is acting like a diesel engine, in which firing takes place without a spark.

Differential A gear system that drives both axles at the same time at different speeds (such as when the car is turning a corner).

Dipstick A flat metal rod used to measure the fluid level in a reservoir.

Disc brakes A brake assembly that uses a caliper with pads to pinch a rotating disc to stop the car. They are used for both front and rear brakes.

Distributor The device within the electrical system that distributes electricity evenly to the spark plugs for efficient combustion.

Distributor cap A plastic insulated cap that covers the distributor mechanism and protects it from moisture and dirt. The cap contains one central terminal surrounded by a group of evenly spaced terminals that distribute secondary voltage to the spark plugs through ignition cables.

Driveline The driveshaft and universal joints that connect the transmission to the rear differential.

Driveshaft The shaft that connects the transmission to the rear axle assembly in a rear-wheel drive car. To ensure flexibility, the driveshaft has at least two universal joints.

Drivetrain   All of the components that generate power and transmit it to the wheels. The drivetrain includes the engine, clutch, transmission, driveshaft, differential, and drive axles.

Drum brakes   A brake system that uses a wheel cylinder to force two brake shoes against the inside of a rotating brake drum to stop the car.

Electrical system   Components that store, generate, and distribute electricity to start and run the car and operate lights and accessories. It consists of the battery, starting circuit, charging circuit, and ignition system.

Electronic fuel injection   A system controlled by computers that injects fuel into the engine's cylinders.

Emergency brake   A secondary brake that is used to lock the car's wheels when it is parked through the use of a mechanical linkage that usually operates only the rear brakes.

Emission controls   A system that cuts down on the emission of harmful gases produced by partly burned fuel, designed to reduce air pollution.

Engine block   A heavy metal block made up of cylinders, pistons, and the crankshaft.

Exhaust manifold   A system that connects the cylinder head exhaust ports to the exhaust pipes, funneling exhaust gases from the cylinders to the pipes.

Fan   A rotating device that draws air through the radiator to increase cooling capacity. Found between the engine and the radiator, it's operated by a belt connected to the crankshaft (or electrically powered), and in most modern cars it operates mostly when the car is idling or driving at a slow speed.

Fan belt   Crankshaft-driven belt that turns the fan.

Filter   A replaceable device used to remove foreign substances from oil, air, or fuel.

Flywheel   A large, heavy wheel that is bolted to the rear of the crank-shaft. The gear on the starter turns the flywheel, which turns the crank-shaft and starts the car. In manual transmissions, the clutch presses against the turning flywheel.

Four-wheel drive   A system in which the engine's power can be delivered to all four wheels.

Front-wheel drive   A system that distributes the engine's power to the front wheels so that the car is pulled by the front wheels instead of pushed by the rear wheels.

Fuel   Any substance that will burn and release heat, such as gasoline, diesel, or propane.

Fuel filter   Fuel system filter that removes particles, contaminants, and some moisture from the car's gas before it gets to the carburetor or fuel-injection system.

Fuel injection   A sophisticated system of computer-controlled fuel delivery that sprays fuel into the air passing through the intake manifold to the cylinders or directly into the cylinders, enriching or thinning the air/fuel mixture before combustion. It is much more efficient than a carburetor.

Fuel line   The part of the fuel system made of rubber, metal, or plastic that transfers gas from the fuel tank to the carburetor or fuel injectors.

Fuel pump   A manual or electrical device used to draw gas from the tank and force it into the fuel system.

Fuel tank   A large steel or plastic compartment usually located in the rear of the car that stores the gas supply.

Fuse   A protective device that interrupts current flow if the circuit becomes overloaded so that other components aren't damaged.

Gap   The space between spark plug electrodes.

Gap gauge   A device used to measure the gap between two surfaces. A thin round strip of wire is used to check the gap between spark plug electrodes to make sure they meet specifications; a thin flat gauge is used to check valve clearance and breaker point gaps.

Gasket   Thin, pliable material made of cork, rubber, or paper used as a seal between two metal parts.

Generator   An electromagnetic device used in older cars that produces electricity when turned. (In newer cars, the alternator does this job.)

Ground   A connection through which electricity flows to complete a circuit.

Head gasket   The seal between the engine block and the cylinder head.

Heater core   A radiator-like unit in which coolant that is used to heat the interior of the car circulates.

Hydraulics   The science of fluid in motion.

Idle speed   How fast the crankshaft rotates in an engine under a no-load condition (out of gear, with no throttle).

Ignition coil   An electrical component used to increase battery voltage in order to fire spark plugs.

Ignition system   The means by which high-voltage electric current is produced and delivered to each spark plug in the combustion chamber.

Independent suspension   A system that allows the left and right wheels to move independently.

Intake manifold   A series of connecting tubes that funnel gas vapor into the combustion chamber.

Internal combustion engine   A type of engine that burns fuel within itself as a way of producing power. As the heated air/fuel mixture expands, it forces a piston downward, turning a crankshaft.

Knock Engine noise caused by detonation or a worn mechanical part, heard when the engine is speeding up or is carrying a heavy load.

Lubrication system The engine system that lubricates and cools engine parts by storing, cleaning, and circulating oil through the engine.

Lug nuts Large steel nuts used to hold a wheel to the axle hub.

Manual steering A type of steering mechanism that doesn't use a power booster.

Manual transmission A type of system (also known as standard or stick shift) in which the driver selects and changes gears using a hand-operated shifting linkage and a foot-operated clutch.

Master cylinder A device that stores brake fluid and forces it through brake lines to each wheel to operate the brakes.

Muffler A chambered device that softens the roar of the engine by funneling exhaust through baffles on its way out of the exhaust system.

Negative terminal A battery terminal (usually black) from which current flows on its path to the positive terminal; it is connected to the ground and usually marked with a minus sign (-) or the word Neg.

Octane Rating indicating a fuel's tendency to resist detonation (pinging); the higher the number, the less it will ping. Octane has nothing to do with the fuel's quality.

Oil filter A canister that contains a filtering device through which oil flows. The filter screens out impurities before the oil circulates through the engine.

Oil pump A small pump in the crankcase that forces oil under pressure from the oil pan through the oil filter to the engine.

Overdrive An arrangement of transmission gears designed to reduce engine speed and increase fuel economy when the car is going above 50 miles per hour (some cars use a fifth gear instead of overdrive).

PCV valve   An emission device that funnels crankcase vapors to the intake manifold to be burned during combustion.

Pinging   Rattling sound heard when you step on the gas, usually associated with pre-ignition of low-octane fuels.

Piston   Cylindrical metal part that is sealed within a hollow cylinder and forced into motion as gas vapors explode. It turns the crankshaft by way of the connecting rods.

Positive terminal   Battery terminal connected to the starter motor and other electrical system connections to which power flows. It is usually marked with a plus sign (+).

Power brakes   Optional type of brakes assisted by a hydraulic or vacuum-operated unit that magnifies the driver's foot pressure during stops, making braking easier.

Power steering   Optional type of hydraulic unit that helps the driver steer the car.

Power train   A group of components that includes the engine, transmission, driveshaft, and rear axle assembly and is used to provide driving force to the wheels.

Rack-and-pinion steering   A light, compact steering system that makes steering more responsive; it replaces the gear box found in older cars.

Radial tire   A popular type of tire with layers or cords set parallel and at right angles to the tire's center.

Radiator   A large chamber in front of the engine that circulates hot engine coolant to cool it off before recirculating to the engine.

Radiator hoses   An upper and lower set of hoses that carry coolant to the radiator to be cooled and circulated back to the engine.

Rear-wheel drive   A type of drivetrain in which the engine's power is transferred to the car's rear wheels.

Rocker arm A lever mechanism under the valve covers that is used to open and close valves in the engine.

Rotor (brake) The disc attached to each wheel in a car with disc brakes.

Rotor (ignition) A device inside the distributor that routes current from the coil to the individual spark plug wires.

Scale Deposits left by contaminants in coolant that can clog passages in the cooling system.

Shock absorber An oil- or gas-filled device at each wheel that controls the bouncing action of the spring devices on the car's suspension.

Spark plug A ceramic and metal part that contains two electrodes; electricity jumps across them to produce a spark, igniting the fuel/air mixture in the cylinder.

Starter A powerful electric motor that spins the engine's flywheel and starts the engine.

Steering system A system of parts that work together to help steer the car, including the steering wheel, steering rack or box, linkage, and front wheels.

Struts A part of the suspension system that contains a damper cartridge and a coil spring; it is used in many cars to replace the shock absorber.

Suspension A group of parts that provides a smooth, shock-free ride by absorbing the car's bouncing action on rough surfaces; it includes the springs, shock absorbers or struts, and steering linkage.

Tie rod One or more rods used to connect steering arms together.

Timing How the valves and ignition system work together (along with other engine parts) to transfer the electrical spark to the spark plug at precisely the right moment for peak engine efficiency.

Timing system   The system that coordinates crankshaft and camshaft rotation so that valves open and close at the right time in conjunction with piston movement. It consists of the timing chain, timing belt, and gears.

Torque   Turning or twisting force.

Transaxle   A transmission and differential combined into one power train unit, used primarily on front-wheel drive cars.

Transmission   A system of gears used to transmit engine power to the wheels.

Tune-up   The periodic process of adjustment and replacement of certain parts as recommended by the car's manufacturer. A tune-up may include timing and carburetor adjustments, spark plug cleaning or replacement, filter replacement, adjustment or replacement of belts, and so on.

Turbocharger   A turbine device that uses exhaust pressure to boost air pressure into the cylinders as a way to increase power.

Universal joint   Also called a U-joint, this flexible joint in a car's drive-shaft allows the shaft to pivot.

Valve   A metal device for opening or closing a port or aperture.

Voltage regulator   A mechanical or electrical device that is used to control the amount of electrical current generated by the alternator.

Water pump   The belt-driven coolant pump on the front of the engine that circulates coolant throughout the radiator and engine.

Wheel bearing   Balls or rollers in heavy grease that allow the wheels to turn without friction.

Wheel cylinder   Hydraulic part at each wheel that forces the brake shoe against the drum in drum brakes and the pads against the rotor in disc brakes.

D

It's Time for Your Reward

Once You've Done This	Reward Yourself
Checked your oil every other fill-up?	Go see the latest movie.
Kept your belts tight and supple?	Enjoy a day at the park with the family.
Rotated tires to even wear?	Take a break with a good book.
Winterized your locks with WD-40?	Enjoy a cup of hot chocolate.
Created a well-lit, safe, working environment?	Sleep in next Saturday.
Acquired a good set of tools?	Spend an afternoon with a friend.
Kept your transmission fluid topped off?	Enjoy a nice cup of tea.
Repaired a tear in your upholstery?	Cuddle up in front of the TV for a great old movie.

Found someone to dispose of used motor oil?

Treat yourself to a favorite meal.

Took off for a long trip with topped-off fluids and a clear conscience?

Enjoy a weekend retreat in the mountains!

Where to Find What You're Looking For

Lock, frozen, 34
Locked out of car, 187–88
Lug nuts, 182, 183

Maintenance, 35–37. *See also*
    Preventive maintenance
    keeping track of, 46–47
    Web sites, 19–20, 22
    worst things you can do, 21,
        47
Manuals, 3–4
Mechanics, 193–95, 198–200
Metric size tools, 4, 28
Mister Fixit, 22
Monthly maintenance, 44–45
Motor oil, 40, 53–56
    changing, 45, 56, 60–61
    checking, 43, 53, 54
    heating in cold weather, 34
    label, understanding, 54–55
    weather and, 55–56
    worst things to do with used,
        53
Mufflers, 79, 135, 138
Mushy brakes, 104
Musty odor smell, 84

National Highway Traffic Safety
    Administration, 18, 19
National Institute for
    Automotive Service
    Excellence, 20, 194
Noises, 76–81, 138, 150
Nutz & Boltz, 21

Octane fuel, 79, 89–90
OEM (original equipment
    manufactured) parts,
    13
Oil. *See also* Motor oil
    gear oil leakage, 85
    hot oil smell, 82
    level, checking, 43, 53,
        54
    spills, 62
Oil pumps, 53–54
Organizations, 17
Organizing tips, 27–32
Overheating, 138, 186–87
Owner's manual, 3–4
Oxygen sensor, 136

Paint, touch-up, 9, 10, 70
Paint job. *See also* Finish of car
    dings, repairing, 69–70
    restoring, 72–73
Park, stuck in, 126–27
Parking brakes, 102
Parts
    maintenance tips, 37
    shopping for, 13–14, 19, 37
PCV filters, 45, 46, 142
PCV valve, 142
Pinging noises, 79
Plugs. *See* Spark plugs
Polish, 10, 67, 72–73
Potholes, 156
Power brakes, 101
Power steering, 146–49
Power steering fluid, 78, 146,
    150
    adding, 153
    checking, 45, 152–53
    leaking, 85, 151–52
Power steering reservoir, 62,
    152, 153
Power train, 123–31
Pressure hose, 146, 151
Preventive maintenance, 43–48,
    51–64
    3 months or 3,000 miles, 45,
        59–63
    weekly, 44, 52–59
Prices of cars, Web sites for,
    18–19
Professional Master Technicians
    Association, 23
Pulling, steering wheel, 149

Quickie service, 198

Rack-and-pinion steering,
    147–48
Radial tires, 63
Radiator. *See also* Coolant
    flushing, 46, 172–73
    maintenance tips, 36
Radiator caps, 167, 188
Radiator hose heater, 33–34,
    170
Radiator neck, 171–72
Rattling noises, 79, 138
Rear clicking, 103

Rear end, 125
Rear suspension, 159–60
Rear-wheel drive, 123, 124
Recirculating ball steering, 148
Repair shops, 194–98
Resonators, 135
Roaring noises, 79
Rod bearing, 76–77
Rotten eggs smell, 83
Running out of gas, 184–85

Safety
    on side of road, 181
    Web sites, 17–18, 19
    when working on car, 38–40
Safety glasses or goggles, 7, 39,
    136, 174
Safety inspections, 46, 143
Salvage yards, 13, 14
Scotchguard™, 10, 70
Screwdrivers, 5, 37
Seat covers, 10, 70
Seats. *See* Upholstery
Service manuals, 3–4
Shimmying, 150
Shock absorber fluid, 85, 156,
    161
Shocks (shock absorbers), 155,
    156–57, 160–61
Singing noises, 80
Slippery road conditions, 35
Slipping clutch, 126
Sluggish performance, 96,
    150–51
Smells, 81–85, 150–51. *See also*
    specific smells
Smoke, 139
Snow, getting stuck in, 185–86
Sockets, 5, 6, 30, 37
Solenoid, 81
Spark plugs, 37, 115–17
Spark plug wires, 117–19
Spark plug wrenches, 5, 116
Specialty repair shops, 197
Springs, 158
Sputtering noises, 97
Squeaking noises, 80
Squeaky brakes, 103
Squealing noises, 80–81
Stalling car, 96, 130
Starter drive, 81

Now you can do these tasks, too!

The Lazy Way

Starting to think there are a few more of life's little tasks that you've been putting off? Don't worry—we've got you covered. Take a look at all of *The Lazy Way* books available. Just imagine—you can do almost anything *The Lazy Way!*

Clean Your House The Lazy Way
By Barbara H. Durham
0-02-862649-4

Handle Your Money The Lazy Way
By Sarah Young Fisher and Carol Turkington
0-02-862632-X

Care for Your Home The Lazy Way
By Terry Meany
0-02-862646-X

Train Your Dog The Lazy Way
By Andrea Arden
0-87605180-8

Cook Your Meals The Lazy Way
By Sharon Bowers
0-02-862644-3

Keep Your Kids Busy The Lazy Way
By Barbara Nielsen and Patrick Wallace
0-02-863013-0

*All Lazy Way books are just $12.95!

additional titles on the back!

Build Your Financial Future The Lazy Way
By Terry Meany
0-02-862648-6

Shed Some Pounds The Lazy Way
By Annette Cain and Becky Cortopassi-Carlson
0-02-862999-X

Organize Your Stuff The Lazy Way
By Toni Ahlgren
0-02-863000-9

Feed Your Kids Right The Lazy Way
By Virginia Van Vynckt
0-02-863001-7

Cut Your Spending The Lazy Way
By Leslie Haggin
0-02-863002-5

Stop Aging The Lazy Way
By Judy Myers, Ph.D.
0-02-862793-8

Get in Shape The Lazy Way
By Annette Cain
0-02-863010-6

Learn French The Lazy Way
By Christophe Desmaison
0-02-863011-4

Learn Italian The Lazy Way
By Gabrielle Euvino
0-02-863014-9

Learn Spanish The Lazy Way
By Steven Hawson
0-02-862650-8